THIS
IS NOT A
HOAX

Urban Legends on the Internet

Karl Wiebe

PublishAmerica
Baltimore

First printing

ISBN: 1-59286-780-4
PUBLISHED BY PUBLISHAMERICA, LLLP
www.publishamerica.com
Baltimore

Printed in the United States of America

Dedication

This book is dedicated to my loving wife Rachelle, who listens to my ideas without laughing, unless I say something funny. I truly appreciate your support and love.

Acknowledgements

This book would not have been possible without the hard work and dedication of many websites that devote their time and energy to debunking myths and legends that society is perpetuating. A full list of the sites that I visited during research is listed in the bibliography at the back of this book, and I also make several references to the better sites throughout the book.

I would like to encourage you to check out their websites and support their sponsors. The internet can be a vast wasteland of poorly run, poorly funded material, or it can be something fun and worthwhile, with great information available for everyone. The future of the internet depends entirely on you. It is important to, in effect, place a vote for these projects, websites and companies with your dollar and with your time.

Introduction

Although many people won't admit it, even to themselves, the fact of the matter is that most of us like a good story more than we like the truth.

Most everyone has heard an urban legend at one time or another. An urban legend is basically a story that is circulated around and refuses to die. "This happened to a friend of a friend," many of them begin.

Most people believe that urban legends are false. While the vast majority of them are indeed not true, there is the odd one that is absolutely true, or based on true events that once happened.

One of the most popular urban legends in the past thirty years is a story that concerns alligators in the New York city sewer system. A few years back, people purchased cute, baby alligators from pet stores and then when the gators grew, they became too much work to look after. The irresponsible owners then slipped them through the sewer openings out on the street at night, or simply flushed the smaller ones down the toilet. Eating garbage and numerous sewer rats, these huge alligators are now roaming the sewer systems, a few feet below the city. Is it true? Could such a fantastic tale actually be based on reality? It depends, according to who you talk to.

Probably the most popular urban legend of our time is the "mysterious hitchhiker" story, which stars a lonely driver on the highway. The details of the story change from region to region around the different countries in the world, but the basics of the tale remain somewhat similar. As the legend unfolds, it is probably raining on a dimly lit highway, as a car speeds along in the night. Suddenly a hitchhiker appears along the side of the road. The driver picks up the hitchhiker. Let's say the new passenger is a young girl, 20 or 21 years old. They chat and drive along, and then suddenly the driver looks over and… the girl is gone! She has disappeared right out of the moving vehicle.

When the shaken driver arrives at the next town, he pulls in to the nearest restaurant and relates his amazing tale to the waitress. She smiles knowingly. That girl had been a hitchhiker who passed away years earlier, in a horrific murder. She has been seen up and down that stretch of highway over the years, striking up conversation and then suddenly vanishing.

Chances are good that you have heard that tale, or something very similar to it at one point in your life. Sometimes it is a horrible automobile accident that determines the fate of the young girl. But did it really happen? Could such a story be true? Impossible! Or is there a chance…

For years and years, most urban legends were told by word of mouth, and the details were often modified to fit the particular country or region that the storytellers lived in. "It happened up that country road over there..." is a popular fixture in many of these tales. But if you were to travel to another region, or another country, a very similar story would occur "just on that country road over the hill, behind the vineyard...".

Because the stories pass from one person to another, and the details change with the region (and decade), the original truths (if any) are almost impossible to verify as absolutely true or false. For decades, the stories slowly migrated around the continent as people moved and travelled.

In recent years, there has been an explosion of rumours, hoaxes, virus warnings, and creepy stories – all thanks to the wonders of modern communication. The progress of the internet by households, and the popularity of email have made it very easy to forward these stories. Some of the legends are the same old legends that have been circulating for decades, but some are quite new and particular to the use of the modern medium.

The purpose of this book is to explore some of the more interesting urban legends that have been circulating in our society, primarily through email and the internet. Let me state right away that this is by no means a comprehensive list of urban legends. There are literally thousands of rumours and legends in our society and others. It is also not the purpose of this book to absolutely prove any particular legend true or false. Urban legends are interesting to read, because it is basically impossible to absolutely prove that the story never happened anywhere on the planet at any time in our history. However, there are many that are so outrageous, it is a safe bet that the story never actually occurred in that exact form.

Basically, the idea for this book grew from the numerous e-mails my co-workers, friends and I would receive while either at work or at home. After about the 50th urban legend crossed my way, I thought about collecting them in a volume that would be accessible to people who did not have e-mail, or chose to read about them in a "non-computer" setting. There are three main advantages to this:

1) I have found that while the computer is a valuable and powerful tool, there are many advantages of books over computers. They are lightweight, small and easy to carry. Books don't need electricity or batteries. And, as long as you can open the cover, they always work properly. I've found that sitting at a computer screen for hours on end is not the most comfortable way to read stories, but with a book, you can choose your own setting.

2) The internet is both vast and unregulated. While all of these stories were found either through email or online, it can be a daunting and frustrating task to find a specific story or theme online. For example, if you type in "September 11" in the Yahoo! search screen, more than 200 reference pages come up. And that's just on one search engine. On some searches, literally thousands of web pages come up, and many of them are duplicates. Which are the "good" ones? People can (and do) spend hours and days researching through page after page of raw data.

3) Much of the content on the internet is written by individuals with no editing or proof-reading whatsoever. From a reader's standpoint, it can be frustrating to read a story with dreadful grammar, bad spelling or HUGE CAPITAL LETTERS to emphasize a point. While I have in fact edited many of the emails I received for the purposes of presenting them in this book, I did on occasion keep the huge capital letters. I might have even kept the "multiple exclamation points!!!!" as well, and for this I make no apologies. Some of these stories are so fantastic, one exclamation point just won't do.

People love great stories, creepy stories, fantastic stories and most of all, stories that *might* be true. Remember, an urban legend does not necessarily have to be false. To be sure, most of them are totally false, and some of them started out based on true stories, but have become horribly distorted over the years. But, some of the stories are absolutely based on true events, or in some rare cases, presented as absolutely true.

If you are interested in any of these urban legends, or stories and legends in general, I would suggest that you check out the internet. It is mind-bending to see the sheer number of hoaxes and stories that are catalogued in these internet databases. There are also newsgroups and discussion forums, where you can not only read about the legends, but also add in your own opinions and thoughts.

The format for this book is simple. I originally gathered up some of the more interesting urban legends I have come across and presented them in no particular order, grouping them into three different categories-

Creepy Stories, which will no doubt make some people lose faith in humanity; *Funny and Outrageous*, which will be much needed to lighten the mood; and *The Almighty Dollar*, with stories that deal mostly with evil corporations and the possibility of someone getting something for nothing.

During the writing of this book, the tragedy and horror of the September 11th attacks in the United States occurred. I was amazed (but not surprised) by the quickness of hoaxes, false prophesies, and downright lies that circulated immediately following the terrorist attacks. I have created a fourth section, simply titled *September 11th*, which showcases the best and the worst that humanity has to offer.

I have also asked a few Internet Technology professionals to present their views on some of the stories, and then of course I often throw my two cents into the fray as well. Some of the urban legends are amusing, funny and weird, and a few of them are downright scary, even if I tell myself that the story is most likely not true. But I hope that you will find all of them interesting and entertaining.

The only criteria I used in deciding which urban legends to include was that it had to be interesting, and that it was passed around by e-mail over the years. One of my favourites is the "rat urine" email that is presented in this book. I had actually received that email more than four years earlier, and it came across my desk again just last week. Like a message in a bottle, bobbing about on the waves in the ocean, these tales continue to beam around the planet, from person to person, through an electric medium.

Let me just state again that this is by no means a comprehensive guide by any stretch of the imagination. I would encourage you to check out the internet for databases that specialize in internet hoaxes, myths, and legends. There are lots out there, and they are very comprehensive and well-researched. While some people are very concerned about whether or not a particular story or true, please note that I really don't care one way or the other. I am presenting these legends as entertainment. Please keep in mind that these are very, very hard to absolutely prove true or false, and that is not my primary intention.

So, throw a log in the fireplace, strike a match and dim the lights. And remember, some of the stories are absolutely true. Or are they?

Creepy Stories

Quit Needling Me!

FW: Safety Bulletin - This is not a joke!

A few weeks ago, in a Dallas movie theatre, a person sat on something sharp in one of the seats. When she stood up to see what it was, she found a needle poking through the seat. There was an attached note saying, "You have been infected with HIV."

The Center for Disease Control in Atlanta reports similar events have taken place in several other cities recently. All of the needles *have* been tested positive for HIV. The CDC also reports that needles have been found in the coin return areas of pay phones and soda machines.

Everyone is asked to use extreme caution when confronted with these types of situations. All public chairs should be thoroughly but safely inspected prior to any use. A thorough visual inspection is considered the bare minimum. Furthermore, they ask that everyone notify their family members and friends of the potential dangers, as well.

The previous information was sent from the Dallas Police Department to all of the local governments in the Washington area and was interdepartmentally dispersed. We were all asked to pass this to as many people as possible.

~ ~ ~

It is definitely scary to think that strangers could be so cruel and heartless.

I originally heard this urban legend back in the mid-80s, before e-mail was a household tool used by millions of people. One of my friends told me that her cousin's boyfriend had done this to one of her friends. But in her version, the boyfriend and the cousin had enjoyed a one-night stand, and then he the next day he left on a plane to Europe. He presented her with a small box that was nicely wrapped. After he boarded the plane, the poor lady opened up her "goodbye gift" and inside was a note that read "You now have AIDS." Remember, back in the mid-eighties, AIDS and HIV were new to the general public. AIDS was mysterious and scary back then (and still is today for many people).

Another version of this myth involves people putting their hands into garbage can receptacles when they throw away paper towels in the bathroom or when people throw away food wrappers in the garbage cans at the mall. There is some truth to this, in that there is a very real danger when you are in public that you could injure yourself. Many warnings about "pushing down" the garbage pile with your bare hands, especially in the bathroom, have been circulating for years. You never know what someone may have disposed before you arrived on the scene.

In regards to the "needle in the seats" scare, the email says that the "information was sent from the Dallas Police Department to all of the local governments in the Washington Area." I checked out the Dallas Police Department website, but there was no mention of this crime. (Check out www.dallaspolice.net for the Dallas Police Department's website).

Did this story actually happen? It is impossible to verify. But there is no harm in inspecting public seats and being careful when disposing of garbage in public places.

Trouble At The Gas Pump

Subject: please read this

A young woman was filling up her car at the local gas station. She paid for her gas, and was returning to her car. Suddenly, the gas station attendant started yelling at her. He shouted that she had not paid him yet. Angrily, the woman went back in to the store to argue about having already paid. Once inside, the attendant told her he just wanted to get her back in the store, because he saw someone crawl in the backseat of her car. He told her not to worry, and that he had already called the police.

This is a true story. It has become a "ritual" of gang members to take one body part from women as an initiation into gangs. The rule is that it has to be in a well lit area and at a gas station, so be careful. The gang members tend to lay under the car and slash the female's ankles when she goes to get into her car. This causes her to fall, and then they cut off a body part, roll and run. They are known to hide behind gas pumps too. It might sound bizarre, but the bigger the body part, the higher the initiation they receive.

This information was communicated by a female law enforcement person that works in the South. She has investigated and been called to a number of these scenes. She has also confirmed the following statement below as true and not an internet "hoax."

Please pass this on to as many people you know, mothers, sisters, grandparents, daughters, nieces and friends. The world, it seems, has become a crazy place to live in. Let's be careful out there and make stuff like this known so we are better protected.

17

It sounds like many gas stations have been informed of this as well, and the attendants are on the watch for such activity. You might want to make a copy of this and hand it to the gas stations you frequent.

~ ~ ~

Again, this is impossible to verify as absolutely true in every detail. However, the truth of the matter is that there are weirdoes out there that can and will take advantage of vulnerable and unaware people.

New Abduction Warnings

Subject: Notes from a friend
A friend of mine sent this to me and I thought it was worth sharing. This is a MUST READ & Please Pass It On...

Recently on *Inside Edition* there was an article about several new scams to abduct women. In one, a man comes up to a woman in a Mall or Shopping Center and asks if she likes pizza. When she says she does, he offers her $100 to shoot a commercial for pizza. However, they need to go outside where the lighting is better. When the woman goes out of the mall she is abducted and assaulted.

Another ploy is the following - a very nicely dressed man asks a woman if she would be in a public service announcement to discourage drug use. The man explains that they don't want professional actors or celebrities. Instead, they are looking for the "average" mother. Once she leaves the mall she is a victim.

The third ploy, and the most successful - a very frantic man comes running in to the mall and asks a woman to please help him. His baby is not breathing. She follows him out of the mall and also becomes a victim. These have been happening in well-lit parking areas, in daylight as well as night time, all over the country. The abductor usually uses a van to abduct the woman.

Inside Edition set up a test in a mall and 10 out of 15 women went out of the mall on the pizza and the public service announcement scam. 100% of the women went out of the mall on the "emergency baby" scam. Please pass this along to your friends and family as now that it has been shown on nationwide TV there are bound to be copycats of this.

The third one, I think, is the scariest. You might resist pizza, or becoming a commercial celebrity... but who would be able to resist a desperate father asking for help for his child? I'm sure that one would get me.

I was going to send this to the ladies only, but guys, if you love your mothers, wives, sisters, daughters, etc., you may want to pass it on to them, as well.

Send this to any woman you know that may need to be reminded that the world we live in has a lot of crazies in it... better safe than sorry.

~ ~ ~

One red flag usually found with urban legends is that the specific information contained in them is usually very hard or even impossible to verify. However, the web site www.urbanlegends.com reports that *Inside Edition* did in fact run a story about 'luring women out of malls' in August 1998. Urbanlegends.com also reported that *Inside Edition* failed to report even such specific incident of a crime in this fashion. Was *Inside Edition* specifically reporting on an actual crime? Or were they merely reporting on an urban legend, and what women could do to protect themselves from such situations or theoretical crimes?

With all due respect to news magazine shows, the majority of them make a living by reporting on the sensational aspects of a story, rather than focusing on just the hard-core journalism. In any event, no one can argue that it is a good idea to be careful when out in public.

The Scary Man At The Mall

A woman was shopping at the Tuttle Mall in Columbus. She came out to her car and discovered that she had a flat. She got her tire jack and spare out of the trunk. A man in a business suit came up and offered to help her. When the tire had been replaced, he asked for a ride to his car on the opposite side of the mall. Feeling uncomfortable about doing this, the woman stalled for a while, but he kept pressing her. She finally asked why he was on this side of the mall if his car was on the other. He claimed he had been talking to friends.

Still uncomfortable, she told him that she had just remembered something she had forgotten to pick up inside the mall and she left him. She made her way back inside the mall, and reported the incident to the mall security. The guard escorted her back out to her car.

The man was nowhere in sight. Opening her trunk, she discovered a briefcase the man had set inside her trunk while helping her with the tire. Inside was a rope and a butcher knife. And later, when she took the tire to be fixed, the mechanic informed her that there was nothing wrong with her tire.

It was flat because the air had been let out of it.

PLEASE BE SAFE AND NOT SORRY! JUST A WARNING TO ALWAYS BE ALERT AND USE YOUR HEAD!

Pass this along to every woman you have access to. Never let your guard down.

~ ~ ~

Well, there really is a mall located at Tuttle Crossing in Columbus, Ohio. (www.shoptuttlecrossing.com). However, the other details of the crime seem very vague.

Scambusters (www.scambusters.org) reported that "Tuttle Mall officials want the public to know that a story about a man threatening a woman in the parking lot is a work of fiction."

Bad Guys at the Mall Again

Beware of someone asking you to purchase perfume. I just wanted to pass this along.

I was approached yesterday afternoon at around 3:30 p.m. in the Wal-Mart parking lot by 2 males asking what kind of perfume I was wearing. I didn't stop to answer them and kept walking toward the store.

At the same time I remembered this email. The men continued to stand between parked cars- I guess to wait on someone else to hit on. I stopped a lady walking toward them, pointed at them, and told her what they might ask and NOT to let them get near her. When that happened, the men and a lady (I don't know where she came from!) started walking the other way toward their car parked in far corner of the parking lot.

~ ~ ~

The threat here is that the two men are going to use some sort of drug to incapacitate the unsuspecting woman in the mall parking lot. Although the locations and details may change somewhat, this sort of thing has definitely happened in North America over the years. Stranger-to-stranger crimes and serial crimes are on the rise, so be on guard and try to avoid areas where you can be vulnerable.

Many police websites feature tips to avoid becoming a target. The following are some of the useful tips from the City of Windsor, Ontario Police Department's website, found at http://www.police.windsor.on.ca:

- Don't display large amounts of money in public nor keep it in the home.
- When in public, always beware of your surroundings. Be mindful of persons loitering or acting suspiciously.
- If you suspect you are being followed, go to the nearest well lit place, populated area, or Block Parent . Yell, if necessary, to attract attention.

Check out your local police department's website, or contact them directly if you have specific questions. Remember, a little bit of paranoia is healthy- it means that you are on guard.

Computer Viruses

There is a new computer virus that is being sent over the internet and through e-mail. If you receive an e-mail message with the subject line "Irina," DO NOT open or read the message. It contains a virus.

Some idiot is sending people files with the title "Irina". If you open the e-mail message, it will rewrite your hard drive, deleting everything on it. Please be careful and forward this message to those you care about!

~ ~ ~

Pretty much everyone with a computer and a modem has received this type of e-mail before. The actual name of the e-mail could be one of hundreds, as could the various damage that it could inflict on your computer. Some e-mails claim that the virus will not only destroy your hard drive, but will jump into the networks at your workplace and latch onto other documents, so that you are not only obliterating your computer, but your co-workers' as well. It is very scary to think that by simply opening up a piece of electronic mail, you are potentially formatting your entire hard drive, effectively destroying your computer.

What is a computer virus? Basically, it is a program that someone has written. A program is just lines of code which execute. Programmers use both small and large programs to run computers. A virus is a destructive program. Instead of the program helping people, it is specifically created to damage computer files and drives.

Have you ever formatted a floppy disk? A programmer could write a program to do just that. And there is nothing necessarily wrong with that. The sinister part of the scenario is when that program is sent in *disguise*, usually through e-mail. You open up your email, not knowing that you are in effect running a program that was designed to format your drive, delete certain files, etc.

Ask anyone who has ever been a victim of a computer virus, and they will probably wince and tell you that it is a very real threat when using the internet, other people's diskettes or computers. I should know. A few years back, when I was in university, I bought a fixer-upper computer from a another student. It was loaded with software, games, applications and all sorts of neat programs. Unfortunately, it did not have virus protection software, and pretty soon after I ran into a nasty virus called "Monkey B".

The Monkey B virus sat in the area of the computer known as the "boot sector," which is one of the very first parts of the hard drive that the computer reads. As soon as the computer booted up, the Monkey B virus basically froze my computer. I was staring at a blank screen. I could override this by "cold booting" my computer, but I had virtually no memory and couldn't run any programs. I could either stare at a blank screen, or cold boot the computer and look at a C-prompt (this was back in the days of MS-DOS).

I finally found an anti-virus program that killed the Monkey B virus. I was able to use my computer again. However, many people have lost valuable documents and in some cases seriously damaged their computer, all due to computer viruses.

A great site for checking out computer virus warnings is http://www.symantec.com/avcenter/hoax.html. This security company has a large listing of false email warnings that commonly circulate at the workplace and home.

The Wizard of Oz Suicide

Subject: Movie Suicide

One of my favourite movies of all time is *The Wizard of Oz*. A friend of mine, who works at a video store, told me about a suicide that occurs right in the movie. At first I didn't believe him, but I rented the movie and watched it at home. He was right! There is an actual suicide in the movie.

He told me that there was a disgruntled actor (one of the Munchkins) and that he was cut from the movie. He hung himself on the set of the movie. No one at the film company noticed the shadow of the suicide and once it made the final cut of the film, it was too late to do anything about it.

Check out the scene right after Dorothy meets the Tin Man, but before they meet the Cowardly Lion. When the three of them say "to Oz" and begin to dance, look over Dorothy's left shoulder. Behind her, you see some movement in the trees. (This is the Munchkin trying to jump off of the platform and hang himself, but it didn't work - he is still alive at this point).

Keep your eye on that area, right in the trees, as they turn around and dance down the yellow brick road. Right when the scarecrow passes the point in the trees, there is a dropping and swinging motion. This is the point where the Munchkin succeeds. His body swings by once before they cut to the next scene.

~ ~ ~

When I read this story, I couldn't believe it. I had seen *The Wizard of Oz* at least ten times, and I couldn't remember seeing anything even remotely like this in the movie. Surely I would have remembered a Munchkin trying to hang himself! I made a mental note to watch this movie again. Incredibly, about two weeks after I read this e-mail, the very same movie was on television, and I taped it.

I had mentioned to my wife Rachelle about the supposed suicide in the movie, but I didn't mention exactly where it occurred, so she wasn't really watching for it. As she was enjoying the movie, I was grimacing, studying the background during the Tin Man scene, hoping I wouldn't miss it.

There is definitely something happening in the background during that scene, and I will be honest – I was a little startled. I basically leapt up from the sofa and pointed at the television. We rewound the tape a bunch of times and watched it again and again, trying to determine exactly what is moving in the shadows in the background.

I went online and looked through chat rooms and web pages, trying to find some definitive proof that this was either in fact a suicide or just an animal or some other movement in the background. I was not able to find any authoritative source that proves this story one way or another. One of the problems I found was that anyone associated with the movie is about eighty years old (or older), and probably they have better things to do with their time than post news in chatrooms or webpages.

There were many arguments online about whether or not the swinging shadow was really a dead body, a peacock, an animal, a stagehand who was not supposed to be there, etc. There is definitely something going on in the back of the scene, but unfortunately it is out of focus and it is basically impossible to decipher what it is. With the rest of the scenery very still, it sure looks out of place, and quite frankly, it is a little creepy to think that there is a dead body hanging in the background while Dorothy and her friends are dancing along to see the Wizard.

Snopes (http://www.snopes2.com), one of the largest internet websites that devotes itself to debunking urban legends, reported that the scene in question was filmed before the Munchkinland scenes, and therefore no Munchkin actors would have been present on the set. This would mean that it would have been impossible for any Munchkin actors to commit suicide during the filming of the forest scene.

A few reports indicate that the movement that we see is in all likelihood a bird. MGM apparently borrowed many live birds from the Los Angeles Zoo to use in the movie. At the very end of the scene, the bird in question flaps its wings. This would make sense and seems a reasonable explanation.

True or False? I would say that it is most likely false. However, the "experts" don't seem to agree entirely on just what is making the mysterious motion in the background.

The Backseat Killer

Subject: lock your car always!

This took place last week right here near downtown. It was after dark, and a woman stopped to get gas at a nearby gas station. She filled her tank and walked into the store to pay for her gas.

The cashier told her not to pay for her gas yet. He instructed her to walk around the store for a little while and act as if she was picking up some other items. Confused, she asked why. The cashier told the woman that a man had just got into the back of her car. He had called the police and they were on their way.

When the police arrived, they found a man in the back seat of the woman's car and asked him what he was doing. He replied that he was trying to join a gang, and the initiation to join was to kidnap a woman and bring her back to the gang to be raped.

According to the police that night, there is a new gang forming right here, that originates from Chicago. Here is the scary part. Because the guy didn't have a weapon on him, the police could only charge him with trespassing. He's back on the streets and free to try again.

Please be aware of what's going on around you, ladies. This could happen to anyone. Please forward this on to anyone you care about!

~ ~ ~

Backseat Killer stories have been around for decades- long before email. Most people write these stories off as mere myths...but are they? There are many police reports over the years of people hiding in, under and around cars, usually with bad intentions. Remember, Ted Bundy used his VW bug quite effectively in his massive killing spree...so while these individual accounts cannot always be tracked down, its always a good idea to look first in the back seat.

I contacted The City of Chicago Police Department and asked them if the above story could possibly be true. This was their response:

The story you reported is almost certainly an 'urban legend.'
Note the vagueness as to date, location, and individual reporting.
Where exactly is 'right here?' We do not usually find offenders who,
when asked what they are doing, volunteer that they are planning to
commit a rape in order to join a gang.

The City of Chicago Police make logical sense. Their website (http://www.ci.chi.il.us/CommunityPolicing/) also features some great safety tips. Some of them are featured below:

- Stay alert at all times and tuned in to your surroundings, wherever you are. The wearing of headphones while walking or jogging can reduce your level of alertness.
- Plan your route in advance, and vary your routes whenever possible.
- Get to know the neighbourhoods and neighbours where you live and work.
- Find out what stores and restaurants are open late and where police and fire stations are located.
- When walking or jogging, use busy streets, and avoid shortcuts through deserted parks, vacant lots, and unlit passages.
- At night, walk or jog only on streets with plenty of light and traffic, and avoid walking alone if possible.
- Walk on the part of the sidewalk close to the street and away from shrubbery, trees, or doorways. On less busy streets at night, it is sometimes safer to walk in the street rather than on the sidewalk.
- Stand tall and walk confidently. Don't make it obvious if you are in unfamiliar territory.
- Trust your instincts. If you feel uncomfortable in a place or situation, leave right away and get help if necessary.

- Women should keep their keys in places other than their purses. That way, if your purse is snatched, you will still have your keys.
- Consider carrying a whistle or other noisemaker, and sound it loudly if you are accosted or feel threatened. Beware of pickpockets, especially in crowded areas.
- Thieves often work in pairs. One may bump you or cut you off, while the other is picking your pocket.
- Before entering an elevator, look at the persons already in the car. If you are uneasy, wait for the next elevator.
- If a suspicious person enters an elevator and you are uneasy, then get off right away.
- If you notice a person in an elevator has not pushed a floor indicator button, do not get off at your floor. Go back to the lobby and report the suspicious activity.
- Stand near the control buttons. If threatened or attacked, sound the alarm and push several floor buttons if possible.

The Flashing Headlights

Subject: Drivers Beware!
One of the police officers who works with the D.A.R.E. program has passed along the following warning and asked that it be shared with all drivers.

This is an extremely serious matter. If you are driving after dark and see a car without its headlights on... DO NOT flash your lights! Do not blow your horn or make any signals to the driver of the other car.

There is a new gang initiation "game" going on in the streets. The new member being initiated into the gang drives along without his headlights on until someone notices and flashes their headlights or makes some sort of other action to signal him. The gang member is then required to chase the automobile and shoot at the car in order to complete his initiation requirements.

Make sure you share this information with your family, friends and anyone else you can reach. If you have any questions or information please call your local police department. Please take this seriously, this is not a joke, please pass this on to everyone you know on e-mail and in person. It could save someone's life.

~ ~ ~

This one is definitely not a new game being played by gang members – this email has been circulating for years. It is easy so see why this myth has endured. It plays on people's fear of strangers. Imagine driving in your car and then suddenly dodging bullets from a crazed gang member.

Should you flash your lights when you see a car without their headlights on? That is an individual choice – although the chance of you saving a life by flashing your lights is probably much greater than the chance of being killed by bullets.

E-mail this...OR ELSE!

THIS IS NOT A JOKE. If you do not forward this e-mail to 20 other people.... Your computer will become a living hell thanks to one of our very own little ingenious viruses. I repeat... this is not a joke! This virus will come to you only a week after you have opened this piece of e-mail. If you open other e-mails after this one, the virus just may come to you disguised as a letter from your "buddy"!

WATCH OUT!

You have one week... starting now.

If this virus gets into your computer, it won't get out. It will slowly delete one file per day. It will start with system IRQ files, startup files, and win95 kernels for registry address (1593338-489h985).

Thank you for your time - ha ha ha ha ha ha ha ha SCREW YOU!!!

~ ~ ~

Again, this e-mail plays on people's fears that they will log on to their computer one morning and discover that their life is ruined. Although computer viruses are very real and do in fact exist, this e-mail above is most definitely a hoax. If you are just sending a letter (text) to someone through e-mail, there is no way (yet) that it can be tracked.

As always, if there is a program file, or an attachment, don't open it unless you are sure of the source. And of course, I would encourage you to run current virus protection software.

True or false? Computer Viruses are definitely true. However, the whole idea of tracking someone's e-mail is currently false.

Many people are nervous about computer viruses because they are not sure what exactly they are. Why would someone go out of their way to create a file that deliberately causes havoc to other people's programs? Is there any foolproof way to protect our data and computers?

There is a great website called "Jeff Richard's Virus and Netlore". It can be found at http://hoaxinfo.com. On his website, he lists "common sense" protection from computer viruses. Some of his tips are summarized below:

1. Viruses are just computer programs. You are in control of what programs run on your computer UNLESS you give that control over to a computer program you receive as an attachment to an email. If you weren't expecting to receive an attachment then it should be immediately suspect! EVEN IF IT IS FROM A FRIEND OR ASSOCIATE YOU TRUST! If you are really determined to check it out check first to see if it is a program file (for Windows users the most common executable files will have an extension of .exe, .bat, .com, .shs, .vbs or .scr and sometimes .jse and .vbe . Just because you get it from a friend you trust doesn't mean it's safe!

2. If you receive an attachment to your email that you can't identify, or if it appears to be a program file from someone you don't know then just DELETE it. You can not get a virus from simply downloading a file. You must run or open the file (by double-clicking on it with your mouse).

3. If you receive an attachment that appears to be a program from someone you trust then by all means scan it for viruses before you click on it using a reliable, up-to-date anti virus program (like Norton or McAfee). Just because your best friend sent it to you NEVER, EVER ASSUME it has been scanned for viruses by them.

4. If you have Microsoft Word on your system there is a special class of malicious code that can be executed by Word automatically when it is opened. Word has the ability to run Word Macro programs which can be embedded in a Word document. These programs run automatically when you open the document. If you receive a Word document (for Window's owners it would have an extension .doc) then scan it with a reliable, up-to-date anti virus program BEFORE opening it.

Final Note: As a general rule, you cannot get viruses from data files. You can safely download and view most picture, movie, or sound files as these are not programs and cannot execute code. Watch out for emails that may tell you a file is a movie file or a sound file. Look at the attachment yourself and if the extension is .exe beware!

LAST WORD OF ADVICE: If you are unsure of what kind of file it is, just apply common sense and delete it!

You Don't Know Jack

Have you ever wondered why they call Jack Daniel's Whiskey "Old Number 7"?

Jack Daniel's Whiskey was originally made in dozens of vats in an old distillery. At some point in time the whiskey from vat number 7 in the distillery started tasting better. It was so good that it was sold as a premium whiskey at a higher price.

After several years, it developed a reputation and was called "Old Number 7." The vats were not cleaned regularly at all- in fact only about every 10 years or so. When vat number 7 was finally cleaned out, a skeleton was found in the bottom.

After doing some research, it was noted that shortly before the whiskey from vat 7 started tasting better, a janitor at the distillery had stopped coming to work. Since he had no family, it was assumed he had moved on to another job.

~ ~ ~

What better way to try to verify this creepy old story than to go to www.jackdaniels.com, a website devoted to the "Old Number 7 Tennessee Whiskey." It is an interesting site, with many facts about Jack Daniel's. For example, did you know that Jack Daniel's Whiskey comes from Lynchberg, Tennessee, a town with a population of just 361 people?

The website makes no mention of a dead janitor or dirty vats. However, they do mention the "No. 7" label on their website:

"Ask 7 different distillery tour guides, and you'll get 7 different stories.

We don't know why Mr. Jack named his whisky Old No. 7, but he must have had a good reason."

Determined to get to the bottom of this mystery, I emailed the company and asked them point-blank to explain the story on Old No. 7.

I was pleasantly surprised by their response. I found the Jack Daniel's company to be very professional and had a good sense of humour. They wrote the following response to me:

We're delighted to hear from you. I'd like to be able to tell you that the story you asked about was true because that would be an interesting story. But the fact is, it isn't true. I don't know how that one got started, but we've had a number of people ask about the janitor falling in the vat. I hope that story never gets back to any of the official tasters because it might tend to make them squeamish! For the record, I can assure you that there are no missing janitors, and we do clean the vats often.

Kind regards,
Jone and friends at Jack Daniel's

Needles on Gas Pump Handles

SUBJECT: DANGEROUS PRANK

Please read this and forward to anyone you know who drives. My name is Captain Abraham Sands of the Jacksonville, Florida Police Department. I have been asked by state and local authorities to write this email in order to get the word out to car drivers of a very dangerous prank that is occurring in numerous states.

Some person has been affixing hypodermic needles to the underside of gas pump handles. These needles appear to be infected with HIV positive blood. In the Jacksonville area alone there have been 17 cases of people being stuck by these needles over the past five months. We have verified reports of at least 12 others in various states around the country. It is believed that these may be copycat incidents due to someone reading about the crimes or seeing them reported on the television.

At this point no one has been arrested and catching the perpetrator(s) has become our top priority. Shockingly, of the 17 people who where stuck, eight have tested HIV positive and because of the nature of the disease, the others could test positive in a couple years. Evidently the consumers go to fill their car with gas, and when picking up the pump handle get stuck with the infected needle.

It is imperative to carefully check the handle of the gas pump each time you use one. Look at every surface your hand may touch, Including under the handle. If you do find a needle affixed to one, immediately contact your local police department so they can collect the evidence.

Please help us by forwarding this email to anyone you know who drives. The more people who know of this, the better protected we can all be.

~ ~ ~

I took a look at the Florida police web pages, and could find no "Abraham Sands" listed in any police jurisdiction. Snopes, the rumour and urban legend website, reports that there is no such police officer, and that this internet legend is false.

It is interesting to note that in these supposed police warnings, there is a lack of details, such as the exact locations of the crimes, the dates and times of the attacks, and any pertinent details that may help citizens to be on the lookout for any wrongdoers. It's basically just a "scare" email that is so vague, that any number of people would assume their own private worst-case scenario.

LSD on the Phone

This is to warn everyone of a new situation happening in communities as a gang initiation and such. Please forward this to anyone you care about immediately, so they can learn of the possible harm. Even if you don't read this, at least forward it to people.

My name is Tina Strongman and I work at a police station, as a phone operator for 911. Lately, we've received many phone calls pertaining to a new sort of problem that has arisen in the inner cities, and is now working its way to smaller towns. It seems that a new form of gang initiation is to go find as many pay phones as possible and put a mixture of LSD and Strychnine onto the buttons.

This mixture is deadly to the human touch, and apparently, this has killed some people on the east coast. Strychnine is a chemical used in rat poison and is easily separated from the rest of the chemicals. When mixed with LSD, it creates a substance that is easily absorbed into the human flesh, and highly fatal.

Please be careful if you are using a pay phone anywhere. You may want to wipe it off, or just not use one at all.

Please be very careful. Let your friends and family know about this potential hazard.

~ ~ ~

Again, this email warning is so vague, that it cannot possibly be legitimate. Where does Tina Strongman work? At a "police station"? Perhaps it would have been a good idea to tell us which police station.

The other hard-to-swallow aspect of this story involves gangs. Most gangs involve kids, or teenagers, and it seems highly unlikely that a group of toughs would be spending their afternoons in some makeshift laboratory, mixing up chemicals for use on public payphones. Wouldn't they rather just go out on the street and rough someone up?

The media usually jumps all over any unusual crime. However, instead of issuing a press release or holding a news conference, Tina Strongman is content to pass around a vague email, warning people of some crime which could be happening in any community in the world. It just doesn't add up.

Trouble at the Bank Machine

Subject: Very scary! Please read...
Whenever you go to an automatic teller machine to make deposits, make sure you don't lick the deposit envelopes. A lady died after licking an envelope at a teller machine at Yonge & Eglinton.

According to the police, Dr. Elliot at the Women's college hospital found traces of cyanide in the lady's mouth and digestive system. The police traced the fatal poison to the glue on the envelope she deposited that day. The police then did an inspection of other envelopes from other teller machines in the area and found six more.

The glue on the envelopes is described as colourless and odourless. They suspect some sicko is targeting this particular bank and has been putting the envelopes beside machines at different locations. A spokesperson from the bank said their hands are tied unless they take away the deposit function from all machines. So watch out, and please forward this message to the people you care about. Spit on the envelopes instead!

~ ~ ~

This email carries the same elements of vagueness that the previous scary crime ones did.

Whether or not this particular instance is true, it is probably a good idea to spit on the envelopes at the bank machines anyway. Who knows how many dirty fingers have touched those envelopes before you arrived.

Ouch! My Kidneys

This is no joke! This story came from the "Daily Texan" - the University of Texas newspaper. Apparently it occurred during Fall Premier - a UT tradition that is a celebration of the end of midterms.

This guy went out last Saturday night to a party. He was enjoying a couple of beers and having a good time. Some girl seemed to like him and invited him to go to another party. He quickly agreed and decided to go along with her. She took him to a party in some apartment and they continued to drink, and even got involved with some drugs.

The next thing he knew, he woke up completely naked in a bathtub filled with ice. He was still feeling the effects of the drugs, but looked around and saw that he was alone. He looked down at his chest, which had "CALL 911 OR YOU WILL DIE" written on it in lipstick.

He saw a phone was on a stand next to the tub. He picked it up and dialed. He explained to the 911 operator that he was sitting in a tub, had taken some drugs and alcohol, and that he didn't know where he was. He didn't know or couldn't remember exactly what he took, or why he was really calling.

The operator advised him to get out of the tub. He stood up, and she asked him to look himself over in the mirror. He did, and he thought he appeared normal. She told him to check his back. He did.

He found two 9-inch slits on his lower back. She instructed him to get back in the tub immediately. A rescue team was on it's way.

Apparently, after being examined, he found out that his kidneys were stolen. They are worth $10,000 each on the black market. (I was unaware this even existed.)

Several guesses are in order: The second party was a sham, the people involved had to be at least medical students, and it was not just recreational drugs he was given. Regardless, he is currently in the hospital on life support, awaiting a spare kidney.

And....

The University of Texas in conjunction with Baylor University Medical Center is conducting tissue research to match the sophomore student with a donor. I wish to warn you about a new crime ring that is targeting business travelers. This ring is well organized, well funded, has very skilled personnel, and is currently in most major cities and recently very active in New Orleans. The crime begins when a business traveler goes to a lounge for a drink at the end of the work day. A person in the bar walks up as they sit alone and offers to buy them a drink. The last thing the traveler remembers is sipping that drink, until they wake up later in a hotel room bath tub, their body submerged to their neck in ice.

There is a note taped to the wall instructing them not to move and to call 911. A phone is on a small table next to the bathtub for them to call. The business traveler calls 911, who by now have become quite familiar with this crime. The business traveler is instructed by the 911 operator to very slowly and carefully reach behind them and feel if there is a tube protruding from their lower back.

The operator knows that both of the business traveler's kidneys have been harvested.

This is not a scam or out of a science fiction novel, it is real. It is documented and confirmable. If you travel or someone close to you travels, please be careful. Sadly, this is very true. My husband is a Houston Firefighter / EMT and they have received alerts regarding this crime ring. It is to be taken very seriously. The daughter of a friend of a fellow firefighter had this happen to her. Skilled doctors are performing these crimes! (Which, by the way have been highly noted in the Las Vegas area).

Additionally, the military has received alerts regarding this. This story blew me away. I really want as many people to see this as possible so please bounce this to whoever you can.

Is this not one of the scariest things you have ever heard of? PLEASE forward this to everyone you know.

~ ~ ~

This is one of my favourite urban legends of all time. It starts out as fantastic and just keeps getting more and more surreal. What a nightmare! By the end of the email, the military are involved, and these crime rings are operating in full force in both New Orleans and Las Vegas.

The moral of the story is pretty obvious. Be careful when in the company of strangers, and be very careful about what you put into your mouth and body. Could it possibly be true?

You can check out the Daily Texan newspaper online at http:www.dailytexanonline.com. This paper has been serving the University of Texas for more than 100 years. They have a huge archive section. I was able to find no original article about the kidney thieves, but there were a few responses by the paper, no doubt frustrated at the deluge of calls that they had received.

Linda Toothman wrote a response to the kidney thieves in the Daily Texan. One would think that such an article, written in the very paper that the kidney-thief urban legend allegedly started, would extinguish the rumours like cold water on burning garbage. But, less than six months later, the Daily Texan had to put out another editorial, in response to the same rumour that refuses to die.

809 Phone Scam

Ok, here's a little pop quiz to test your dialling IQ; Which of the area codes below is located in the U.S., where domestic long-distance rates would apply?

a) 809
b) 758
c) 664
d) 242
e) 868
f) 473
g) 902
h) 709
i) 869
j) 345

Answer: none of them. They are all international calls, each of them billed at a different rate based on carrier and international agreements. And calling them could lead to a phone bill of hundreds of dollars. The area codes are:

809: Dominican Republic
758: St. Lucia
664: Montserrat
242: Bahamas
868: Trinidad and Tobago
473: Grenada
902: Nova Scotia

709: Newfoundland
869: Nevis/St. Kitts
345: Cayman Islands

Here's how the scam works. First, you get an urgent e-mail or phone message asking you to call a special number (usually beginning with 809) to win a prize, settle an outstanding account, or alert you of an ill relative. When you call the number, someone at the other end puts you on hold. A month later you get hammered with a huge charge on your phone bill.

What makes this so clever, and the reason why it works, is that you don't have to dial 011 to reach certain countries. But there are locations outside the United States, many of them in the Caribbean, where you simply dial the area code and number to reach your party. And there are scam artists who have taken advantage of this confusion by promoting calls to "809" numbers in the Dominican Republic. While these telephone numbers may look like domestic long distance calls, international telephone rates apply.

SPECIAL ALERT. DO NOT EVER DIAL AREA CODE 809. Don't respond to emails, phone calls or pages which tell you to call an "809" phone number.

This scam has also been identified by the National Fraud Information Center and is costing victims a lot of money. There are lots of different permutations of this scam, but here is how it works.

Permutation #1: You receive an email, typically with a subject line of "ALERT" or "Unpaid Account." The message, which is being scammed across the net, says: I am writing to give you a final 24 hours to settle your outstanding account. If I have not received the settlement in full, I will commence legal proceedings without further delay. If you would like to discuss this matter to avoid court action, call Mike Murray at Global Communications at 1-809-496-2700.

Permutation #2: You receive a message on your answering machine or your pager which asks you to call a number beginning with area code 809. The reason you're asked to call varies: It can be to receive information about a family member who has been ill, to tell you someone has been arrested, died, or to let you know you have won a wonderful prize, etc.

In each case, you're told to call the 809 number right away. Since there are so many new area codes these days, people unknowingly return these calls. If you call from the US, you will apparently be charged $25 per minute!

Sometimes the person who answers the phone will speak broken English and pretend not to understand you. Other times, you'll just get a long recorded message. The point is, they will try to keep you on the phone as long as possible to increase the charges. Unfortunately, when you get your phone bill, you'll often be charged more than $100.00.

Here's why it works- the 809 area code is located in the British Virgin Islands, in the Bahamas. The 809 area code can be used as a "pay-per-call" number similar to 900 numbers in the US.

Since 809 is not in the US, it is not covered by US regulations of 900 numbers which require that you be notified and warned of charges and rates involved when you call a "pay-per-call" number. There is also no requirement that the company provide a time period during which you may terminate the call without being charged. Further, whereas many US phones have 900 call blocking (to avoid these kinds of charges), 900 number blocking will not prevent calls to the 809 area code.

We recommend that no matter how you get the message, if you are asked to call a number with an 809 area code that you don't recognize, make sure to investigate further and/or disregard the message. Be very wary of email or calls asking you to call an 809 area code number. It is important to prevent becoming a victim of this scam, since trying to fight the charges afterwards can become a real nightmare. Disputing the charges can be very difficult, since you actually made the call. If you complain, both your local phone company and your long distance carrier will not want to get involved and will most likely tell you that they are simply providing the billing for the foreign company. You'll end up dealing with a foreign company that argues that it has done nothing wrong.

Please forward this entire email to your friends, family and colleagues to help them become aware of this scam – don't get ripped off.

~ ~ ~

This email sounds far-fetched, but parts of it are in fact true. In North America, there are "1-900" numbers that charge the customer fees (like $2.00 per minute, for example). The 809 area code scam works in a similar fashion. But it is important to point out that there are many 809 area code numbers that are legitimate. The part of the email that advises you to "never call an 809 number" is false. If a phone number happens to have an 809 area code, that doesn't automatically make it a "pay per minute" phone number.

A great website that explores this scam further is www.scambusters.org. It is also very good advice to phone a phone number only if you know who is going to answer the phone at the other end. A little research often goes a long way.

The Parisian Bellboy

An American family of four went to Paris, France on vacation. The family checked into a hotel and then went sightseeing and shopping.

A few days into their pleasant, normal vacation, the family went for lunch at a café. Upon returning to their hotel room that afternoon, they were shocked to discover that their hotel room had been broken into. Fortunately, it seemed to have been a rather surgical strike and very few of their possessions were stolen. In fact, hardly anything was even out of place. Two things, however, struck the family as odd- their four toothbrushes are strewn around the sink, and their camera was set out in the open on one of the beds.

The hotel manager was apologetic and blamed the bellboy. The bellboy, who had seemed so nice to the family upon their arrival, had just quit his job on the morning of the break-in.

The Americans got the missing portion of their traveller's cheques refunded, checked into a new hotel, wound up their vacation and headed back to America.

In America, they developed the pictures in the camera. Half of them were of the family in front of the Eiffel Tower, but the other half of the pictures in the roll featured various views of the bellboy, smiling deliriously, with the four family toothbrushes stuck up his booty.

~ ~ ~

This one was so disgusting, there is really nothing I can add. Except, of course, that this urban legend is actually true, according to postings made at

52

http://www.urbanlegends.com. If you check out their website, there is a "classics" section and under "Parisian Bellboy" you can see emails from people who claim to have actually seen the photos in question. Sometimes it is hotel workers from Mexico, other times it is employees from Europe, but people claim that this has actually happened.

It is interesting to note that in some instances, the urban legend or myth becomes so well known that people actually begin to perform the very same urban legend that they believe to be true. A good (and less disgusting) example of this is the "garden gnome" prank that has been around for decades. Basically, the practical joke goes like this: someone, embarking on a trip around the world, runs over to his neighbour's yard and steals a garden ornament or little gnome. The neighbour wakes up, goes out to get his newspaper and discovers the theft. Weeks pass, and the gnome is long gone. However, one fateful day, the neighbour receives an ominous and mysterious package in the mail. It is a letter from Europe... and it is signed "The Gnome"! There is usually a picture of the gnome in front of the Eiffel Tower, or the Taj Mahal, or wherever the gnome thief happens to be at the time. Sometimes the gnome is returned, and sometimes the thief keeps the ornament, as a reminder of the prank.

This gag has been around for years- long before the internet in fact. The story of the gnomes has become somewhat of a self-fulfilling prophecy. People wonder if the "gnome" urban legend is truly real, and the fact of the matter is that since so many people have heard of it, people continue to steal gnomes. And, apparently, toothbrushes.

Blush Spider

Three women in Chicago turned up at hospitals over a 5 day period, all with the same symptoms. They all had a fever, chills, and vomiting, followed by muscular collapse, paralysis, and finally, death. There were no outward signs of trauma. Autopsy results showed toxicity in the blood. These women did not know each other, and seemed to have nothing in common. It was discovered, however, that they had all visited the same restaurant (Big Chappies, at Blare Airport), within days of their deaths.

The health department descended on the restaurant, shutting it down. The food, water, and air conditioning were all inspected and tested, but to no avail. Finally the big break came when a waitress at the restaurant was rushed to the hospital with similar symptoms. She told doctors that she had been on vacation, and had only went to the restaurant to pick up her paycheque. She said that she did not eat or drink while she was there, but she had used the restroom.

That is when one toxicologist, remembering an article he had read, drove out to the restaurant at the airport, went into the restroom, and lifted the toilet seat. Under the seat, out of normal view, was small spider. The spider was captured and brought back to the lab, where it was determined to be the South American Blush Spider (arachnius gluteus), so named because of its reddened flesh colour.

This spider's venom is extremely toxic, but can take several days to take effect. They live in cold, dark, damp, climates, and toilet rims provide just the right atmosphere.

Several days later, a lawyer from Los Angeles showed up at a hospital emergency room. Before his death, he told the doctor that he had been away on business and had taken a flight from New York. He had changed planes in Chicago before returning home. He did not visit Big Chappies while there. He did, as did all of the other victims, have what was determined to be a puncture wound, on his right buttock.

Investigators discovered that the flight he was on had originated in South America. The Civilian Aeronautics Board (CAB) ordered an immediate inspection of the toilets of all flights from South America, and discovered the Blush spider's nests on 4 different planes.

It is now believed that these spiders can be anywhere in the country. So please, before you use a public toilet, lift the seat to check for spiders.

It can save your life! And please pass this on to everyone you care about

~ ~ ~

For those who don't like spiders, this doesn't help. Fortunately, I could not find confirmation of these stories online, but I did find a few vehement denials of the airport restaurant, and even the species of spider in general. Chances are that this email is completely untrue. However, it is always good advice to inspect anything in public places before exposing bare skin.

Another Virus Warning

Subject: Virus alert

Hi everyone,

A virus has been passed on to my computer. As your contact is in my address book, you may have received this virus from me as well. Please see the instructions below to delete and pass on to your contacts.

The virus (called jdbgmgr.exe) is not detected by Norton or McAfee or VET anti virus systems. The virus sits quietly for 14 days before damaging the system. It's sent automatically by messenger and by the address book whether or not you send e-mails to your contacts. Here's how to check for the virus and how to get rid of it.

YOU MUST DO THIS :

1. Go to start (bottom left corner), find the search option (or "find").
2. In the files / folders option, write the name jdbgmgr.exe
3. Be sure to search your C: drive and any other drives you may have.
4. Click "find now"
5. The virus has a teddy bear icon with the name jdbgmgr.exe DO NOT OPEN IT.
6. Go to edit : choose "select all" to highlight the file without opening it.
7. Now go to file and select "delete". It will go to your recycle bin.
8. Go to your recycle bin and delete it there as well.

IF YOU FIND THE VIRUS YOU MUST CONTACT ALL THE PEOPLE IN YOUR ADDRESS BOOK SO THEY CAN ERADICATE IT IN THEIR OWN ADDRESS BOOKS. SORRY ABOUT THIS.
I'M SURE EVERYONE IN THE ADDRESS BOOK WILL HAVE IT. To do this:

- open new email message, click the photo of the address book next to TO.
- Click every name and add to BCC.
- Copy this message, enter subject, paste to email, send.

Sorry about this. Just found out about this now. I did find the virus sitting contently on my computer. If you follow the steps you can delete quite easily. I'm sorry about this. I do a virus scan weekly and still these things get through.

~ ~ ~

I received this email from a person I had never recognized. Why was my address sitting in her inbox? It seemed strange.

This virus warning is completely false. The reason that you have the jdbmgr.exe file is that it was installed when Microsoft Windows was installed on every computer with a Windows operating system. If you delete this file, you are deleting a normal executable file from your system.

There is a good site that details this and other virus hoaxes: http//securityresponse.symatec.com

If you receive virus warnings at work, make sure to check with your IT professional. Do NOT delete any files unless they give you the OK. Trying to "fix" your own computer often causes more trouble than if you just leave it to the professionals.

Flesh Eating Bananas

Subject: URGENT warning
Dear Friend,
Please forward to everyone you love!
This is VALIDATED FROM THE CDC. (Center for Disease Control in Atlanta, Georgia).

Several shipments of bananas from Costa Rica have been infected with necrotizing fasciitis, otherwise known as flesh eating bacteria. Recently this disease has decimated the monkey population in Costa Rica. We are now just learning that the disease has been able to graft itself to the skin of fruits in the region, most notably bananas, which are Costa Rica's largest export.

Until this finding scientists were not sure how the infection was being transmitted. It is advised not to purchase bananas for the next three weeks as this is the period of time for which bananas that have been shipped to the US with the possibility of carrying this disease. If you have eaten a banana in the last 2 or 3 days and come down with a fever followed by a skin infection, seek medical attention.

The skin infection from necrotizing fasciitis is very painful and eats two to three centimetres of flesh per hour. Amputation is likely. Death is possible.

If you are more than an hour away from a medical center, burning the flesh ahead of the infected area is advised to help slow the spread of the infection.

The FDA has been reluctant to issue a country wide warning because of fear nationwide panic. They have secretly admitted that they feel upwards of 15,000 Americans will be affected by this but that these are acceptable numbers.

Please forward this to as many people you care about as possible as we do not feel 15,000 people is an acceptable number.

~ ~ ~

Again, I could find no confirmation of this story. And it has been circulating around on the internet for years, so who knows what "two to three week" period they are referring to. The details of the above email are very vague, and as I found out below, completely false.

The CDC (Centre for Disease Control) issued the following press release in January 2000, which would seem to directly contradict the urban legend.

False Internet report about necrotizing fasciitis associated with bananas

The bacteria which most commonly cause necrotizing fasciitis frequently live in the human body. The usual route of transmission for these bacteria is from person to person. Sometimes, they can be transmitted in foods, but this would be an unlikely cause for necrotizing fasciitis. FDA and CDC agree that the bacteria cannot survive long on the surface of a banana.

For information about necrotizing fasciitis, check CDC's website at http://www.cdc.gov/ncidod/dbmd/diseaseinfo/#G. Look under "Group A Streptococcus" which is the most common cause of necrotizing fasciitis. Or, call (404) 371-5375.

Kentucky Fried... Something

Subject: KFC NOTICE

KFC has been a part of our American traditions for many years. Many people, day in and day out, eat at KFC regularly. Do they really know what they are eating? During a recent study of KFC done at the University of New Hampshire, they found some very interesting facts.

First of all, has anybody noticed that just recently, the company has changed their name? Kentucky Fried Chicken has become KFC. Does anybody know why? We thought the real reason was because of the "fried" food issue.

It's not.

The reason why they call it KFC is because they can not use the word chicken anymore. Why?

KFC does not use real chickens. They actually use genetically manipulated organisms. These so called "chickens" are kept alive by tubes inserted into their bodies to pump blood and nutrients throughout their structure. They have no beaks, no feathers, and no feet.

Their bone structure is dramatically shrunk to get more meat out of them. This is great for KFC because they do not have to pay so much for their production costs. There is no more plucking of the feathers or the removal of the beaks and feet. The government has told them to change all of their menus so they do NOT say chicken anywhere. If you look closely you will notice this. Listen to their commercials. I guarantee you will not see or hear the word chicken.

I find this matter to be very disturbing. I hope people will let other people know. Please forward this message to as many people as you can. Together we make KFC start using "real" chicken again.

~ ~ ~

This email is completely outrageous, especially if one logically thinks it through. The costs involved in genetically engineering a beakless chicken with no feet and shrunken bone structure would be astronomical, as would the hardware (tubes and fluids) for feeding these weird creatures. Wouldn't it be much easier and less expensive to feed regular chickens bags of feed? I would think so.

Also, there are thousands of people involved in the meat plants, cutting and trimming chickens in preparation for their restaurants. Are we to seriously believe that no one has come out of the woodwork to speak up on this? How come no one has seen this on the news? I would think it would make for some juicy headlines, pardon the pun. The people working in the meat plants aren't high-level government officials working on some top-secret military campaign.

Many people love conspiracies, and the exciting thought of the federal government keeping this secret from the public is one of the reasons that this email gets circulated around on a regular basis.

And of course, to top it all off, I watched a KFC commercial on the television and the announcer in the commercial used the word "chicken" repeatedly.

Klingerman Virus

Subject: Very Serious Information!!!

This is an alert about a virus in the original sense of the word...one that affects your body, not your hard drive.

There have been 23 confirmed cases of people attacked by the Klingerman Virus- a virus that arrives in your real mail box, not your email in-box.

Someone has been mailing large blue envelopes, seemingly at random, to people inside the USA. On the front of the envelope in bold black letters is printed, "A gift for you from the Klingerman Foundation." When the envelopes are opened, there is a small sponge sealed in plastic.

This sponge carries what has come to be known as the Klingerman Virus. Public health officials state this is a strain of virus they have not previously encountered.

When asked for comment, Florida police Sergeant Stetson said, "We are working with the CDC and the USPS, but have so far been unable to track down the origins of these letters. The return addresses have all been different, and we are certain a remailing service is being used, making our jobs that much more difficult."

Those who have come in contact with the Klingerman Virus have been hospitalized with severe dysentery. So far, seven of the twenty-three victims have died. There is no legitimate Klingerman Foundation mailing unsolicited gifts.

If you receive an oversized blue envelope in the mail marked, "A gift from the Klingerman Foundation", DO NOT open it. Place the envelope in a strong plastic bag or container, and call the police immediately.

The "gift" inside is one you definitely do not want.

PLEASE PASS THIS ON TO EVERYONE YOU CARE ABOUT.

~ ~ ~

The Center For Disease Control in Atlanta confirmed that the "Klingerman" virus is definitely not real. The CDC ask website viewers to not forward any emails concerning the Klingerman virus. However, they do advise people to contact their local post office if you are concerned about a suspicious package, or if you are worried about what may be in a package that you receive. They also advise that it is a criminal offence to try to deliberately cause harm to someone, even if it is in the mail.

Cocaine Baby

Subject: SAD STORY

Please pass this story on after reading it. Everyone needs to know about this. My sister's co-worker has a sister in Texas, who was planning a weekend trip with her husband across the Mexican border for a shopping spree.

At the last minute their baby sitter cancelled, so they had to bring along their two-year-old son. They had been across the U.S./Mexico border for about an hour when their baby boy got free and ran around the corner. The mother went chasing after him, but the boy had disappeared. The mother quickly found a police officer. The officer told her to go to the gate and wait. She didn't really understand the instructions, but she did as she was told.

About 45 minutes later, a stranger approached the border carrying the boy. The mother ran to the man, grateful that her son had been found. When the man realized it was the boy's mother, he dropped the boy and fled. The police were waiting for him and apprehended the stranger. Her son, however, was dead.

In the 45 minutes or so that the boy was missing, he was cut open. All of his insides were removed and his body was stuffed with cocaine.

The man was going to carry the boy across the border as if he were asleep. A two-year-old boy, dead, discarded as if he were a piece of trash for somebody's cocaine. If this story can get out and change one person's mind about what drugs mean to them, we are helping.

Please send this E-mail to as many people as you can. Let's hope and pray it changes a lot of minds. The saddest thing about the whole situation is that those persons who suffer are innocents - people we love.

~ ~ ~

I could find no credible confirmation of this story. However, I did come across some postings, as well as an informative article by David Emery (a writer and internet legend debunker). You can view the article in its entirety by going to

http://urbanlegends.miningco.com/library/weekly/aa092198.htm

There he reports that the urban legend dates back to the 1970s, and was reported as true in the *Washington Post* in the 1980s. However, the *Washington Post* later printed a retraction, stating that they could not substantiate their story and that it was in fact untrue.

You can also check out http://hoaxinfo.com, which basically agrees that the *Washington Post* reported the story incorrectly. Apparently the media are susceptible to being fooled as well.

Lethal Rat Urine

A stock clerk was sent to clean up a storeroom at their Maui, Hawaii location. When he got back, he was complaining that the storeroom was really filthy, and that he had noticed dried mouse or rat droppings in some areas.

Just a couple of days later, he started feeling like he was coming down with a stomach flu - he had achy joints, a headache, and he started throwing up. He went to bed and never really got up. Within two days he was deathly ill. His blood sugar count was down to 66 and his face and eyeballs were yellow. He was rushed to the emergency at Pali Momi, where they said he was suffering from massive organ failure. He died shortly before midnight.

None of us would have ever made the connection between his job and his death, but the doctors specifically asked if he had been in a warehouse or exposed to dried rat or mouse droppings at any time. The doctors said there is a virus (much like Hanta virus) that lives in dried rat and mouse droppings. Once dried, these droppings are like dust, and can easily be ingested if a person is not careful to wash their hands and face thoroughly, or wear protective gear.

An autopsy was conducted to verify the doctors' suspicions. This is why it is extremely important to ALWAYS carefully rinse off the tops of any canned sodas or foods, and wipe off pasta packaging, cereal boxes, etc.

Almost everything you buy in a supermarket was stored in a warehouse at one time or another, and stores themselves often have rodents. Most of us remember to wash vegetables and fruit, but almost never think of the dust on boxes and cans. The ugly truth is that even the most modern, upper-class, superstore can have rats and mice. And their warehouse most assuredly does.

~ ~ ~

This urban legend is certainly one of the most popular, and it would seem fairly reasonable to assume that package foods, including soft drinks, would be stored in warehouses. But could rats really be touching food that we eat?

It is definitely true that the packaged food that we eat often comes from far away. You can imagine some food being processed in Europe or Asia, and it would be packaged, sit in a warehouse, then make its way to a port city, where it would be loaded on board a huge barge, spend many days on the ocean as it crosses the sea to North America, and then sit in a port city's warehouse for a number of days until it is finally shipped to a local grocery store or even yet another warehouse. There are many chances for animals and vermin to come in contact with food. Even clean warehouses and storage facilities have rats and mice. It is inevitable in larger, older buildings.

The part of the email that would appear to be exaggerated regards the severity of coming into contact with rat droppings or urine. Hantavirus Pulmonary Syndrome (HPS) and Leptospirosis are both diseases that people can get if they come into contact with rat urine. However, these instances are extremely rare (generally less than 250 cases per year in the United States - or basically a one in a million chance) and usually people need repeated exposure to dried rat droppings or urine. Even then, HPS and Leptospirosis are treatable if they are properly diagnosed.

Exposure to rat urine and feces is not necessary deadly or even harmful, provided that the animal is healthy. Leptospirosis is passed from diseased animals to humans- it is not inherently found in all rats or animals.

Generally speaking, regular bacteria or e-coli pose a greater threat to your health when you are drinking a soda pop. The advice of washing the tops of soda cans is sound, however. It is always a good idea to wash your hands when preparing food, and to wash produce such as vegetables and other "touchable" food items.

Snopes.com is one of the best urban legend websites out there, and they dug a little deeper into the story. According to the email, the victim of the rat urine was working in Maui, and then was "rushed to Pali Momi" ER. However, the Pali Momi hospital is 75 miles away, on another island. Are you telling me that there are no medical facilities on all of Maui? Unlikely. But such details aside, it is still good advice to wash the tops of soda cans. Even if it just contains dust and a bit of dirt, who wants to touch that with their mouth?

More Rat Urine

Whenever you buy any canned juice or soft drink, please make sure that you wash the top with running water and soap. If that is not available, drink your beverage with a straw. A family friend's friend died after drinking a can of soda!

A brief investigation by the Center for Disease Control in Atlanta discovered the cause. The top was encrusted with dried rat's urine which is toxic and obviously lethal!

Canned drinks and other food stuffs are stored in warehouses. The boxes and containers that are usually infested with rodents and then get transported to the retail outlets without being properly cleaned.

Please forward this message to the people you care about.

~ ~ ~

Again with the rat urine. Rat urine is not "obviously" toxic and lethal. According to the Center For Disease Control in Atlanta (found at www.cdc.gov):

- People generally get Leptospirosis by coming into contact with water that contains urine from animals with the disease.
- People generally get infected with the disease from coming into contact with contaminated water, food or soil that contains the infected urine from these sick animals.
- It takes about 2 days to 4 weeks to show symptoms of being sick with Leptospirosis. Symptoms include fever, chills, headache and diarrhea.

- Recovery from this disease may take days to several months.
- Leptospiroris is treated with antibiotics.
- If Leptospiroris is not treated, it can lead to kidney failure, meningitis, or liver failure.

The CDC makes no mention of Leptospiroris being lethal. However, logic would dictate that if a person were to become horribly ill, not have it treated, and suffered liver or kidney failure, then this could kill a person.

Of course, the urban legends emails don't tell you the facts. It is much more exciting to visualize someone taking a sip of their beverage and basically dropping dead within 24 hours.

The Worst Taco Ever

TRUE STORY:
This girl was really in a hurry one day, so she just stopped off at a Taco Bell and got a chicken soft taco and ate it on the way home. That night she noticed her jaw was kind of tight and swollen. The next day it was a little worse. Finally she went to her doctor.

The doctor said she just had an allergic reaction to something, and gave her some cream to rub on her jaw to help. After a couple of days the swelling had gotten worse- she could hardly move her jaw. She went back to her doctor to see what was wrong.

Her doctor had no idea why her jaw was getting worse, so he started to run some tests. They scrubbed out the inside of her mouth to get tissue samples and they also took some saliva samples. Well, they found out what was wrong.

Apparently her chicken soft taco had a pregnant roach in it. When she ate it, the eggs somehow got into her saliva glands. Over the past week she had been incubating them. The doctors had to remove a couple a layers of her inner mouth to get all the eggs out. If the medical staff hadn't figured out what was going on, the eggs would have hatched inside the lining of her mouth.

She's suing Taco Bell (of course).

~ ~ ~

This tale certainly seems far-fetched. Even in the extremely unlikely event that a "pregnant roach" was found in a taco, how could it possibly get into a person's saliva glands? Is such a thing even possible?

It seems highly unlikely, although I am sure that some people are convinced that this sort of thing could happen. It is virtually impossible to guarantee that all of our food will be free of insects or other such creatures. But even in the event that roach eggs ever get into your mouth, it is even more unlikely that they would be able to survive. Remember, saliva is part of your digestive system, which is designed to break down organic matter (which in effect kills it).

Oh Susanna – Creepy Guy

There were two roommates - Sarah and Megan. Sarah was the theatrical type. She loved acting. She was in all the town's plays. Megan was more of a book person- she loved to read and her studies were her first priority.

There was a huge play called *Oh, Susanna* that Sarah was in, and it was coming up on Saturday. Every chance that Sarah got, she would practice in the park. She said that that's where she got her inspiration. Sarah would practice for hours. Every time, she would beg Megan to go with her, but Megan would stay in the dorm and read.

Saturday came and Sarah was a hit. Being the star, she was detained after the play, and got home really late. As she entered, she heard her roommate's rocking chair squeaking in the corner, but couldn't see it, as almost all of the lights were off. *Hmm, must be waiting for me*, Sarah thought. Putting her stuff away, she went back into the main room.

From the corner came a voice. It sounded rather husky, but that wasn't what agitated Sarah.

"Oh, Susanna, don't you cry for me..." came the voice.

"Stop it Megan! Don't give me that crap, okay?" said Sarah.

"Oh, Susanna, don't you cry for me..."

"Stop!"

"Oh, Susanna, don't you cry for me..."

"Stop it! I mean it, Meg!"

"Oh, Susanna, don't you cry for me..."

"*Stop! That's it!*" Sarah screamed as she flicked on the room's lights.

Sarah gawked in horror at the sight. Her roommate's body was in the rocking chair, but her head wasn't. Megan's head was on the wall, kept there by a butcher knife. From behind the rocking chair she could hear laughter – maniacal laughter.

"Who's there? *Who are you?*"

From behind the rocking chair jumped a man, later found out to be the butcher that escaped from the sanitarium in the next town. All the time he was cutting Sarah, he was singing, over and over, "Oh, Susanna, don't you cry for me... I come from Alabama with a banjo on my knee."

Pinning Sarah to the wall next to her roommate's head, he screamed, "Now, Susanna, don't you cry for me!"

~ ~ ~

This one is so melodramatic, vague and corny that I almost put it in the "Funny and Outrageous" section. However, real people have escaped from prison and medical facilities, so I suppose at least some of the elements of this story could be true. Make sure to lock the doors when you are sitting at home alone at night!

Roaches in the Glue

A woman was working in a post office in California. One day she licked the envelopes and postage stamps instead of using a sponge. That very day the lady cut her tongue on the envelope. A week later, she noticed an abnormal swelling of her tongue. She went to the doctor. The doctor checked her over, but he found nothing wrong. Her tongue was not sore, so she didn't really worry about it.

A couple of days later, her tongue started to swell more, and it began to get really sore. It was irritating her so badly that she could not eat. She went back to the hospital and demanded something be done.

The doctor took an x-ray of her tongue, and noticed a lump. He prepared her for minor surgery. When the doctor cut her tongue open, a live roach crawled out.

It turns out that there were roach eggs on the seal of the envelope. The egg was able to hatch inside of her tongue, because of her saliva. It was warm and moist.

I used to work in an envelope factory, and I can speak from experience. The storage facilities are crawling with roaches. They are all over the envelopes. Don't put any in your mouth!

~ ~ ~

This one sounds so absurd, but in fact could have a grain of truth to it. I came across some postings online from people who have worked in glue factories (or at least claim to) and they have said that there are in fact roaches in this environment.

Licking envelopes might not be the most sanitary thing to do, but it is unlikely that you would get seriously ill from it. Again, your saliva is designed to break down organic matter, so it is probable that eggs would not survive in that environment.

The Forest Fire

Subject: The Worst Day Ever
THIS IS A TRUE STORY.
The next time you think you are having a bad day, remember the following story. After a recent forest fire in California, the authorities were assessing the damage and came across a burned corpse.

The deceased was an adult male dressed in a full wet suit, complete with a SCUBA tank on his back and flippers. He was even wearing a face mask.

The post-mortem revealed that the man died from massive internal injuries. The authorities were understandably confused. Investigators set out to determine just how a fully-suited SCUBA diver ended up in the middle of a raging forest fire.

It was revealed that on the day of the fire, the SCUBA diver went for a dive off the coast, some 25 miles away. The firefighters had called in a fleet of helicopters, equipped with large dip buckets. The helicopters dipped from the nearby ocean and then flew to the blaze to help put out the raging inferno.

~ ~ ~

This certainly makes for a good case of the shivers, but there is no evidence that this story ever actually took place. Apparently this legend has been circulating since the 1980s, and is a favourite among divers. However, the logic behind it seems flawed; the apparatus used for a helicopter to pick up the water is rather small and it would be an awful long shot to pick up an adult male, especially wearing full SCUBA gear. In other versions of the same story, it is a super-scooper airplane that sucks up our unfortunate diver.

The typical size of the bucket opening on the helicopter in question is about one foot (twelve inches). It would be impossible for even a small child in SCUBA gear to be pulled into one of these machines.

Bombardier water bombers have two intakes for water, and they are both four inches by ten inches. Besides the small size, the water intakes have grills on them.

Check out www.fantasyscuba.com as well for a non-urban legend website that reports on this story. It can find no instance of this story being true. However, it does mention that a diver was injured once due to the eddies (currents) caused by a helitanker that was reloading. In Corsica, the currents caused by the helitanker knocked the diver against a landing stage. The diver suffered a bruised leg but was otherwise alright.

This story is a great example of a tale so outrageous and shocking that most people secretly want it to be true. The urge to tell this one is very strong, despite their being no evidence that it ever happened.

The Car Wreck on Hwy 69

This story takes place many years ago, in the late 30's or early 40's. It happened not far from McAlester, OK. A vehicle was driving down Highway 69 and approached a bridge. The driver and his friend looked out his window and saw wreckage down below, near the river. He pulled over and scurried down the bank to the river, hoping to be of some help to anyone who might be alive. He found a young woman, bruised and cut up - but still alive.

They dragged her out of the wreckage and helped her out of the crashed car. She asked about her baby. One of the men searched for the infant but could not find any sign of him. Later, a search party searched for several hours but only turned up the infant's blanket.

Nowadays, if you go out to the bridge after dark and park your vehicle, leaving your engine running, lights on, radio playing, anything on the vehicle running at all, sooner or later your vehicle will die. Everything will shut down completely. Even your watch, if you happen to be wearing one, will stop running.

After several minutes you will hear a baby begin crying. The crying will be ever so faint at first, then grow louder until it sounds as if it is in the vehicle with you. Then suddenly it will stop. Your vehicle will start running once again, as will anything that you had running before.

~ ~ ~

This is a good story, but completely impossible to absolutely verify. There are simply no details in the story to substantiate or debunk. There is a location, but no date and no names. If in fact this story were true, then it would be absolute proof of the supernatural, which would be one of the greatest news stories of all time. So it seems unlikely that this story is the "best kept secret" online.

Is Someone Watching You?

HOW TO DETECT A 2-WAY MIRROR
When we visit toilets, bathrooms, hotel rooms, changing rooms, or the like, how many of you know for sure that the seemingly ordinary mirror hanging on the wall is a real mirror. Could it actually be a 2-way mirror (i.e., they can see you, but you can't see them)?

There have been many cases of people installing 2-way mirrors in female changing rooms. It is very difficult to positively identify the surface by just looking at it. So, how do we determine with any amount of certainty what type of mirror we are looking at? Just conduct this simple test:

Place the tip of your fingernail against the reflective surface and if there is a GAP between your fingernail and the image of the nail, then it is a GENUINE mirror. However, if your fingernail DIRECTLY TOUCHES the image of your nail, then BEWARE, FOR IT IS A 2-WAY MIRROR!

So remember, every time you see a mirror, do the "fingernail test."

~ ~ ~

Now you can't even go into the change room without the fear of some stranger peeping at your private parts. The really sad part of this story is that there really are two-way mirrors, and people really may be watching you when you are not aware. Even if you choose to believe that the two-way mirror is completely preposterous, substitute in the phrase "video camera" and suddenly it is doubly-creepy.

We live in a society that enjoys watching each other. That means that sometimes you are the recipient of someone else's gaze, even if you are not aware of it.

Funny and Outrageous

!?

Good Times Virus

(Editor's note: The credit given below was the credit that was displayed on the version that I received.)

Written by Patrick J. Rothfuss, December 1996:
READ THIS:
Goodtimes will re-write your hard drive. Not only that, but it will scramble any disks that are even close to your computer. It will recalibrate your refridgerator's coolness setting so all your ice cream goes melty. It will demagnetize the strips on all your credit cards, screw up the tracking on your television and use subspace field harmonics to scratch any CD's you try to play.

It will give your ex-girlfriend your new phone number. It will mix Kool-aid into your fish tank. It will drink all your beer and leave its socks out on the coffee table when there's company coming over. It will put a dead kitten in the back pocket of your good suit pants and hide your car keys when you are late for work.

Goodtimes will make you fall in love with a penguin. It will give you nightmares about circus midgets. It will pour sugar in your gas tank and shave off both of your eyebrows while dating your girlfriend behind your back and billing the dinner and hotel room to your Discover card.

It will seduce your grandmother. It does not matter if she is dead - such is the power of Goodtimes. It reaches out beyond the grave to sully those things we hold most dear.

It moves your car randomly around parking lots so you can't find it. It will kick your dog. It will leave libidinous messages on your boss's voice mail in your voice! It is insidious and subtle. It is dangerous and terrifying to behold. It is also a rather interesting shade of mauve.

Goodtimes will give you Dutch Elm disease. It will leave the toilet seat up. It will make a batch of Methanphedime in your bathtub and then leave bacon cooking on the stove while it goes out to chase gradeschoolers with your new snowblower.

Listen to me. Goodtimes does not exist.

It cannot do anything to you. But I can. I am sending this message to everyone in the world. Tell your friends; tell your family. If anyone else sends me another e-mail about this fake Goodtimes virus, I will turn hating them into a religion. I will do things to them that would make a horsehead in your bed look like Easter Sunday brunch.

~ ~ ~

The message with the "Good Times" virus is pretty simple. Think before you click. A little bit of research, such as checking out the urban legend online (such as www.snopes.com or www.urbanlegnds.com), could stop a potential deluge of emails from clogging up servers and annoying friends.

Cool Video Clip Chain Letter

OK here's the deal, this works. I don't know how... but it works.

You have to send this email to no less than 11 people. Somehow, from the return path generated, you'll receive... something, and it is funny!

This is the coolest thing I've ever gotten! All you have to do is send it to 11 people and this little video comes up on your screen and shows the funniest clip. I can't tell you what it is but I was laughing so hard! So spend a few seconds to send this and you'll be glad you did! Thanks!

~ ~ ~

This one simply does not work. It is one of the most annoying emails to receive, because the person sending it usually includes a line like "Well, no harm done. I had to try!" Yes, there is harm done. To my sanity.

One of the most annoying traits about most people in the world is that people LOVE to tell others about cool stuff. So why would the author of this email NOT tell you what it is exactly that you are going to see? It just doesn't make sense.

Internet Cleanup Day

Subject: Internet Cleanup Day
THIS MESSAGE WILL AGAIN BE REPEATED IN MID-FEBRUARY.
* * * Attention * * *
It's that time again!

As many of you know, each year the Internet must be shut down for 24 hours in order to allow us to clean it. The cleaning process, which eliminates dead email and inactive ftp, www and gopher sites, allows for a better working and faster internet.

This year, the cleaning process will take place from 12:01 a.m. GMT on February 27 until 12:01 a.m. GMT on February 28 (the time least likely to interfere with ongoing work). During that 24-hour period, five powerful internet search engines situated around the world will search the Internet and delete any data that they find.

In order to protect your valuable data from deletion, we ask that you do the following:

1. Disconnect all terminals and local area networks from their Internet connections.
2. Shut down all internet servers, or disconnect them from the Internet.
3. Disconnect all disks and hard drives from any connections to the Internet.
4. Refrain from connecting any computer to the Internet in any way.

We understand the inconvenience that this may cause some Internet users, and we apologize. However, we are certain that any inconveniences will be more than made up for by the increased speed and efficiency of the Internet, once it has been cleared of electronic flotsam and jetsam.

We thank you for your cooperation.

~ ~ ~

It is hard not to laugh when reading this one. Anyone with any sort of common knowledge about the internet immediately recognizes this to be false. However, that has not stopped this sort of e-mail from circulating for years. Why is that?

This email plays on people's fears that by connecting their computer through a phone line, they will somehow wind up with a deleted hard drive. The internet technology might no longer be new, but there are thousands of new and inexperienced users everyday logging on. Many of these people are unsure and naïve.

Once you start looking in detail at the e-mail, it is easy to see that it is not only false, but pretty silly. It is pretty much impossible to get every single server in the world to simultaneously shut down for 24 hours. And which federal government has the authority to go rummaging through the global internet, deleting any files, in any country, that they find? Remember that the internet is a collection of people's web pages and information. No one owns it, and no one can control it.

True or False? Absolutely False. If you get this e-mail message, delete it and forget about it.

SULFNBK - You Are Your Own Worst Enemy

Dear Friends,

We have been unwittingly just infected with a virus from someone's email.

THIS Klez Worm VIRUS SENDS ITSELF TO ALL THE ADDRESSES IN THE ADDRESS BOOK OF THE COMPUTER IT HAS ARRIVED AT. Take the time and remove it now. The instructions are easy and I got rid of it in a few minutes. Some versions of anti virus software including Norton and Inoculate T have not been able to detect it. It is said that the virus HIDES in the computer for 2 weeks and then DAMAGES THE DISC IRREPARABLY.

The virus is called sulfnbk.exe Many apologies for the trouble it is causing.

Go to "Start" and click on "Find" or "Search".

In the box, "find files or folders" type in sulfnbk.exe (the name of the virus)

Make sure you are searching in the C-drive (check in the box marked "Search in").

Click on Find

If the file is found you will find an ugly black icon with the name sulfnbk.exe This file is a program. DO NOT OPEN IT.

Click on the RIGHT button of the mouse, on the file name, and then click on DELETE with the LEFT BUTTON OF THE MOUSE.

You will be asked to send this file to the recycle bin or wastebasket---respond YES.

Open the recycle bin and eliminate the file, manually or by emptying the entire recycle bin or wastebasket.

If you do find this virus in your computer, send this email to all the people in your address book because the virus is transmitted in this way. (Even if you don't find the virus, you should probably still send this email to all your addresses).

I thought this was a joke at first but it is not and we found the ugly icon when we followed the above directions. Good luck!

~ ~ ~

This email is a complete hoax. There really is a file on your computer called SULFNBK.EXE. However, its not a virus. It is a Microsoft Windows utility that allows the computer to restore long file names. Basically, people should just leave this file alone. If they delete it, your computer may encounter problems regarding file names.

The www.symantec.com website includes versions of the hoax in English, French, Chinese, Swedish, Spanish, Portugese, and other languages. It is a hoax that is huge in scale and has been disrupting people's computers for quite a while.

Very Bad Luck?

CASE 1: Kelly Sedey had one wish: for her boyfriend of three years, David Marsden, to propose to her. Then one day when she was out to lunch David proposed! She accepted, but then had to leave because she had a meeting in 20 minutes.

When she got to her office, she noticed on her computer she had e-mail. She checked it. It was the usual stuff from her friends. But then she saw one that she had never gotten before. It was this letter. She simply deleted it without even reading all of it.

BIG MISTAKE! Later that evening, she received a phone call from the police. It was about DAVID! He had been in an accident with an 18 wheeler. He didn't survive.

CASE 2: Take Katie Robbenson. She received this letter and, being the believer that she was, she sent it to a few of her friends but didn't have enough e-mail addresses to send out the full 10 that you must. Three days later, Katie went to a masquerade ball.

Later that night when she left to get to her car to go home, she was killed on the spot by a hit-and-run drunk driver.

CASE 3: Richard S. Willis sent this letter out within 45 minutes of reading it. Not even 4 hours later, walking along the street to his new job interview with a really big company, he ran into Cynthia Bell, his secret love for 5 years. Cynthia came up to him and told him of her passionate crush that she had had on him for two years.

Three days later, he proposed to her and they got married. Cynthia and Richard are still married with three children, happy as ever!

This is the letter:

Around the corner I have a friend,
In this great city that has no end,
Yet the days go by and weeks rush on,
And before I know it, a year is gone.
And I never see my old friends face,
For life is a swift and terrible race,
He knows I like him just as well,
As in the days when I rang his bell.
And he rang mine if, we were younger then,
And now we are busy, tired men.
Tired of playing a foolish game,
Tired of trying to make a name.
"Tomorrow" I say "I will call on Jim"
"Just to show that I'm thinking of him."
But tomorrow comes and tomorrow goes,
And distance between us grows and grows.
Around the corner!- yet miles away,
"Here's a telegram sir" "Jim died today."
And that's what we get and deserve in the end.
Around the corner, a vanished friend.

Remember to always say what you mean. If you love someone, tell them. Don't be afraid to express yourself. Reach out and tell someone what they mean to you. Because when you decide that it is the right time, it might be too late.

Seize the day. Never have regrets. And most importantly, stay close to your friends and family, for they have helped make you the person that you are today.

You must send this on in 3 hours after reading the letter to 10 different people. If you do this, you will receive unbelievably good luck in love. The person that you are most attracted to will soon return your feelings.

If you do not, bad luck will rear its ugly head at you.

THIS IS NOT A JOKE! You have read the warnings, seen the cases, and the consequences. You MUST send this on or face dreadfully bad luck.

NOTE The more people that you send this to, the better luck you will have.

~ ~ ~

There are two types of people in this world - ones who believe in "luck" and those who don't.

There is no logical explanation of how sending an e-mail to your friends is connected to good or bad luck. But many people are superstitious, or believe in fate, and agree wholeheartedly that "what goes around comes around". That would explain why this vague and ominous letter has been making the rounds. Note near the end of the email, the reader is reminded that they have "read the warnings, seen the cases, and the consequences." What have we seen? There is no possible way to substantiate anything written in the email. Who are these people? Where do they live? How is there any connection to their demises? Are there any people who didn't read the email, deleted it, and survived? Logic would say that at least three people on the entire planet could have deleted this email without forwarding it and not have been killed or suffered some such unfortunate ending. Even if you could find those three other people, that would reduce your probability of death to 50%. This is obviously not an objective email.

Apparently the message here is that we are supposed to "seize the day" and "stay close to friends and family". Would it not make more sense to spend your time with those you care about instead of sitting at a computer reading this email? I'm still not sure why we should "read alone", as it asks at the start of the letter. I guess you don't need any of your annoying friends bothering you while you read a letter about friendship?

Neiman Marcus Cookie Recipe

Subject: Free Neiman-Marcus Cookie Recipe
This is a true story... Please forward it to everyone that you can....
You will have to read it to believe it....

My daughter and I had just finished a salad at Neiman-Marcus Cafe in Dallas & decided to have a small dessert. Because both of us are such cookie lovers, we decided to try the "Neiman-Marcus Cookie".

The cookie was so good that I asked the waitress if she would give me the recipe. She frowned and said, "I'm afraid not."

"Well," I said, "would you let me buy the recipe?"

"Yes," she said with a cute smile.

I asked how much it would be and she responded, "only two fifty-it's a great deal!"

I said with approval, "just add it to my tab."

Thirty days later, I received my Visa statement from Neiman-Marcus and it was **$285.00**. I looked again and remembered I had only spent $9.95 for two salads and about $20.00 for a scarf. As I glanced at the bottom of the statement, it said, "Cookie Recipe - $250.00". I thought, "that's outrageous!"

I called Neiman's Accounting department. I told them that the waitress said it was "two-fifty," which clearly does not mean "two hundred and fifty dollars" by any reasonable interpretation of the phrase.

Neiman-Marcus refused to budge.. They would not refund my money, because according to them, "what the waitress told you is not our problem. You have already seen the recipe - we absolutely will not refund your money at this point."

I explained to her the criminal statutes which govern fraud in Texas. I threatened to refer them to the Better Business Bureau and the State's Attorney General for engaging in fraud. I was basically told, "do what you want- we don't give a damn and we're not refunding your money."

I waited a moment, thinking of how I could get even, or even try to get any of my money back. I just said, "okay, you folks got my $250, and now I'm going to have $250 worth of fun."

I told her that I was going to see to it that every cookie lover in the United States with an e-mail account has the $250 cookie recipe from Neiman-Marcus... for **free**.

She replied, "I wish you wouldn't do this!" But I said, "well, you should have thought of that before you ripped me off!", and slammed down the phone.

So, here is the recipe! Please, please, please pass it on to everyone you can possibly think of. I paid $250 dollars for this... I don't want Neiman-Marcus to ever get another penny off of this recipe!

2 cups butter
4 cups flour
2 tsp. baking soda
2 cups granulated sugar
2 cups brown sugar
5 cups blended oatmeal (measure oatmeal and blend in blender to a fine powder)
24 oz. chocolate chips
1 tsp. salt
1 8 oz. Hershey bar (grated)
4 eggs
2 tsp. baking powder
3 cups chopped nuts (your choice)
2 tsp. vanilla

Cream the butter and both sugars. Add eggs and vanilla; mix together with flour, oatmeal, salt, baking powder, and soda. Add chocolate chips, Hershey bar and nuts. Roll into balls and place two inches apart on a cookie sheet. Bake for 10 minutes at 375 degrees. Makes 112 cookies. Have Fun!

~ ~ ~

This is one of the oldest and most popular of the internet urban legends. However, it appears that it is completely false. The recipe for the Neiman Marcus Cookies are found on Neiman Marcus' own website, http://www.neimanmarcus.com. The website says to "copy it, print it out, pass it along to friends and family. It's a terrific recipe. And it's absolutely free."

Neiman Marcus also apparently only accepts American Express and their own Neiman Marcus credit card. So the "Visa" aspect of the story would also appear to be false.

There is a similar urban legend that circulated much earlier (before the internet) in the 1930s. The story goes that a lady stayed at the Waldorf Astoria Hotel in New York. While dining, she ate a piece of Red Velvet cake and enjoyed it so much that she asked for the recipe. When she received her hotel bill, she was shocked to find that she had been charged one hundred dollars. (Back in the 1930s, during the depression, that would have been quite a surprise to find on a bill).

Sweet, Sweet Revenge

For all of you who occasionally have a really bad day when you just need to take it out on someone! Don't take that bad day out on someone you know. Take it out on someone you DON'T know!

Now get this. I was sitting at my desk when I remembered a phone call I had to make. I found the number and dialled it. A man answered nicely, saying "Hello?" I politely said, "This is Patrick Hanifin. Could I please speak to Robin Carter?"

Suddenly the phone was slammed down on me! I couldn't believe that anyone could be that rude. I must have had the wrong number. I tracked down Robin's correct number and called her.

She had transposed the last two digits incorrectly. After I hung up with Robin, I spotted the wrong number still lying there on my desk. I decided to call it again. When the same person once more answered, I yelled "You are a jackass!" and hung up. Next to his phone number I wrote the word "jackass," and put it in my desk drawer.

Every couple of weeks, when I was paying bills, or had a really bad day, I'd call him up. He'd answer, and I'd yell, "You're a jackass!" It would always cheer me up.

Later in the year the phone company introduced caller ID. This was a real disappointment for me. I would have to stop calling the jackass. Then one day I had an idea. I dialled his number, then heard his voice.

"Hello," he said.

I made up a name. "Hi there. This is the sales office of the telephone company and I'm just calling to see if you're familiar with our caller ID

98

program?" He shouted "No!" and slammed the phone down.

I quickly called him back and said, "That's because you're a jackass!"

The reason I took the time to tell you this story, is to show you how if there's ever anything really bothering you, you can do something about it. Just dial 823-4XX3.

(Editor's note: I deleted out part of the number)

Keep reading, it gets better.

The old lady at the mall really took her time pulling out of the parking space. I didn't think she was ever going to leave. Finally, her car began to move and she started to very slowly back out of the slot. I backed up a little more to give her plenty of room to pull out. *Great*, I thought. *She's finally leaving.* All of a sudden, a bright red Camaro came flying up the parking isle in the wrong direction and pulled into her space. I started honking my horn and yelling, "You can't just do that, buddy. I was here first!"

The guy climbed out of his Camaro, completely ignoring me. He walked toward the mall as if he didn't even hear me. I thought to myself, *This guy's a jackass. There sure a lot of jackasses in this world.*

I noticed he had a "For Sale" sign in the back window of his Camaro. I wrote down the number. Then I hunted for another place to park. A couple of days later, I was at home, sitting at my desk. I had just gotten off the phone after calling 823-4863 and yelling, "You're a jackass!". (It was really easy to call him now since I have his number on speed dial.)

I noticed the phone number of the guy with the red Camaro lying on my desk and thought I'd better call this guy, too. After a couple rings someone answered the phone and said, "Hello."

I said, "Is this the man with the red Camaro for sale?"

"Yes, it is."

"Can you tell me where I can see it?"

"Yes, I live at 1802 West 34th street. It's a yellow house and the car's parked right out front."

I said, "What's your name?"

"My name is Don Hansen."

"When's a good time to catch you, Don?"

"I'm home in the evenings."

"Listen Don, can I tell you something?"

"Yes."

"Don, you're a jackass!" And I slammed the phone down.

After I hung up I added Don Hansen's number to my speed dialler. For awhile things seemed to be going better for me. Now when I had a problem I had two jackasses to call. Then, after several months of calling the jackasses and hanging up on them, it just wasn't as enjoyable as it used to be. I gave the problem some serious thought and came up with a solution.

First, I dialled Jackass #1. A man answered nicely saying, "Hello."

I yelled "You're a jackass!", but I didn't hang up.

The jackass said, "Are you still there?"

I said, "Yeah."

He said, "Stop calling me."

I said, "No."

He said, "What's your name, Pal?"

I replied, "Don Hansen."

He said "Where do you live?"

"1802 West 34th Street. It's a yellow house and my red Camaro's parked out front."

"Oh Yeah? Well, I'm coming over right now, Don. You'd better start saying your prayers."

"Yeah, like I'm really scared, Jackass!" and I hung up.

Then I called Jackass #2.

He answered, "Hello."

I said, "Hello, Jackass!"

He said, "If I ever find out who you are..."

"You'll what?"

"I'll kick your butt!"

"Well, here's your chance. I'm coming over right now Jackass!"

And I hung up.

Then I picked up the phone and called the police. I told them I was at 1802 West 34th Street and that I was going to kill my gay lover as soon as he got home. Another quick call to Channel 13 about the gang war going on down W. 34th Street. After that I climbed into my car and headed over to 34th Street to watch the whole thing.

Glorious!

Watching two Jackasses kicking the crap out of each other in front

of 6 squad cars and a police helicopter was one of the greatest experiences of my life!
Name withheld to protect the guilty.

~ ~ ~

Either you love this one or you just shake your head. This one is so far-fetched, it is absolutely ridiculous. There are way too many coincidences for it to be even remotely plausible. (For example, it is very convenient that the guy with the Camaro has a "For Sale" sign on his car.)

The whole story is a great work of fiction, but I would be extremely surprised if it was even partially true. (Except for the guy stealing the parking spaces. That happens all too often, I am afraid.)

Archaeological Findings

A woman who works at Mattel Toy Co. as a cost engineer on Barbie dolls forwarded this one on through the net...

The story behind this letter is that, apparently there is a nutball who digs things out of his backyard and sends his "discoveries" to the Smithsonian, labeling them with scientific names and insisting they are actual archaeological finds. This guy really exists and does this in his spare time. Anyway, what follows is a letter from the Smithsonian in response to his submission of a recently discovered specimen.

Dear Sir:

Thank you for your latest submission to the Institute, labelled "211-D, layer seven, next to the clothesline post. Hominid skull." We have given this specimen a careful and detailed examination, and regret to inform you that we disagree with your theory that it represents "conclusive proof of the presence of Early Man in Charleston County two million years ago."

Rather, it appears that what you have found is the head of a Barbie doll, of the variety one of our staff, who has small children, believes to be the "Malibu Barbie."

It is evident that you have given a great deal of thought to the analysis of this specimen, and you may be quite certain that those of us who are familiar with your prior work in the field were disappointed to come to contradiction with your findings.

However, we do feel that there are a number of physical attributes of the specimen which might have tipped you off to it's modern origin:

1. The material is moulded plastic. Ancient hominid remains are typically fossilized bone.
2. The cranial capacity of the specimen is approximately 9 cubic centimetres, well below the threshold of even the earliest identified proto-hominids.
3. The dentition pattern evident on the "skull" is more consistent with the common domesticated canine (dog) than it is with the "ravenous man-eating Pliocene clams" you speculate roamed the wetlands during that time. This latter finding is certainly one of the most intriguing hypotheses you have submitted in your history with this institution, but the evidence seems to weigh rather heavily against it.

Without going into too much detail, let us say that:

A. The specimen looks like the head of a Barbie doll that a dog has chewed on.
B. Clams don't have teeth.

It is with feelings tinged with melancholy that we must deny your request to have the specimen carbon dated. This is partially due to the heavy load our lab must bear in its normal operation, and partly due to carbon dating's notorious inaccuracy in fossils of recent geologic record. To the best of our knowledge, no Barbie dolls were produced prior to 1956 AD, and carbon dating is likely to produce wildly inaccurate results.

Sadly, we must also deny your request that we approach the National Science Foundation's Phylogeny Department with the concept of assigning your specimen the scientific name "Australopithecus spiff-arino." Speaking personally, I, for one, fought tenaciously for the acceptance of your proposed taxonomy, but was ultimately voted down because the species name you selected was hyphenated, and didn't really sound like it might be Latin.

However, we gladly accept your generous donation of this fascinating specimen to the museum. While it is undoubtedly not a hominid fossil, it is, nonetheless, yet another riveting example of the great body of work you seem to accumulate here so effortlessly. You should know that our Director has reserved a special shelf in his own office for the display of the specimens you have previously submitted to the Institution, and the entire staff speculates daily on what you will happen upon next in your digs at the site you have discovered in your back yard.

We eagerly anticipate your trip to our nation's capital that you proposed in your last letter, and several of us are pressing the Director to pay for it. We are particularly interested in hearing you expand on your theories surrounding the "transpositating fillifitation of ferrous ions in a structural matrix" that makes the excellent juvenile Tyrannosaurus Rex femur you recently discovered take on the deceptive appearance of a rusty 9-mm Sears Craftsman automotive crescent wrench.

Yours in Science,
Harvey Rowe

~ ~ ~

This is a funny story, and there are no doubt instances of people digging things up in their backyard and thinking that their find is of great scientific value, only to find that it was in fact an ordinary (and not ancient) item.

Unfortunately, this story does not appear to be true either. Steve Platt, in his article "Archaeology on the Web" (http://www.channel4.com/history/timeteam/archonweb10.html) debunks the story. There is no "Harvey Rowe" working at the Smithsonian, and he claims that it all began back in 1994 when a South Carolina student wrote a funny story for his friends.

Microwave and Water: Beware!

Subject: Microwave and Water

I feel that the following is information that anyone who uses a microwave oven to heat water should be made aware of.

About five days ago my 26-year-old son decided to have a cup of instant coffee. He took a cup of water and put it in the microwave to heat it up. He had done this numerous times before. I am not sure how long he set the timer for but he told me he wanted to bring the water to a boil.

When the timer shut the microwave oven off, he opened the door and removed the cup. As he looked into the coffee mug, he noted that the water was not boiling but instantly the water in the cup "exploded" into his face. The cup remained intact until he threw it out of his hand but all the water had exploded out into his face due to the buildup of energy. His whole face is blistered and he has 1st and 2nd degree burns which may leave scarring. He also may have lost partial sight in his left eye.

While at the hospital, the attending doctor stated that this a fairly common occurrence and water, by itself, should never be heated up in a microwave oven. If water is heated in this manner, something should be placed in the cup to diffuse the energy such as a wooden stir stick or tea bag.

It is however a much safer choice to boil the water in a tea kettle. Please pass this information on to friends and family.

~ ~ ~

This sounds incredible, but there appears to be some confirmations that this in fact can happen. It all seems to stem from the science behind the microwave oven heating up liquid differently than a regular stove does. I am not a science expert by any stretch of the imagination, but what follows is basically what I was able to piece together. As with all of these urban legends, if any of them fascinates you, there are many articles and in-depth analyses online.

When water heats up on the stove, the heat is coming from a super-hot element (the burner) that heats up the liquid. But it heats up only the bottom of the pot, and in fact the bottom of the pot is hotter than 100 degrees Celsius. This creates bubbles, and the water only "boils" at the places where the water touches the gas.

In a microwave, radiation heats up molecules. The liquid water gets quite hot, but the container (plastic) that is designed for use in the microwave oven will not get as hot. There are no "boiling bubbles" that are evident when heating water on the stove top. Approximately all of the water gets heated up at the same time. In a microwave oven, the water can become "super heated," in which the water is above the boiling point, but has no opportunities to bubble. (A few bubbles appear, but not the steady stream of bubbles that are evident on the stovetop.)

One really dangerous experiment that illustrates the power of microwaved water is to superheat the water in the microwave oven and then pour in some powder (like sugar). This causes a great number of tiny bubbles which instantly expand and explode.

Make sure that when you heat up water in the microwave, there are other agents in there as well, such as a wooden stick, a teabag, or some other "energy absorbing" matter. And be careful!

This Is Freaky!

Subject: This is freaky!
You'll never know if you don't try...Ok guys, this truly is freaky, the phone literally rang as soon as I read the last word of this email!!!
I am taking the bait - what do I have to lose right?
Hope it works!

Supposedly The Phone Will Ring Right After You Do This.
Just read the little stories and think of a wish as you scroll all the way to the bottom. There is a message here - then make your wish.

Stories

I'm 13 years old, and I wished that my dad would come home from the army, because he'd been having problems with his heart and right leg. It was 2:53 p.m. When I made my wish. At 3:07 p.m. (14 minutes later), the doorbell rang, and there my Dad was, luggage and all!!

I'm Katie and I'm 20 and I've been having trouble in my job and on the verge of quitting. I made a simple wish that my boss would get a new job. That was at 1:35 and at 2:55 there was an announcement that he was promoted and was leaving for another city. Believe me...this really works!!!

My name is Ann and I am 45 years of age. I had always been single and had been hoping to get into a nice, loving relationship for many years. While kind of daydreaming (and right after receiving this email) I wished that a quality person would finally come into my life. That was at 9:10 AM on a Tuesday. At 9:55 AM a FedEx delivery man came into my office. He was cute, polite and could not stop smiling at me. He started coming back almost every day (even without packages) and asked me out a week later. We married 6 months later and now have been happily married for 2 years.

What a great email it was!! Just scroll down to the end, but while you do, think of a wish. Make your wish when you have completed scrolling. Whatever age you are, is the number of minutes it will take for your wish to come true. (Example: You are 25 years old; it will take 25 minutes for your wish to come true).

However, if you don't send this to 5 people in 5 minutes, you will have bad luck for years!!

Go for it!!!
SCROLL DOWN!

```
********************
********************
********************
********************
********************
********************
********************
********************
********************
```

STOP!!!
Congratulations!!! Your wish will now come true in your age minutes.

Now follow this carefully....it can be very rewarding!!!!
If you send this to 10 more people, something major that you've been wanting will happen.
Message: This is scary!
The phone will ring right afteryou do this!

~ ~ ~

There are some major characteristics to these types of urban legends. Virtually all of them are designed to illicit emotions. After reading it, many readers are either angered, fearful, happy, laughing or just plain amused. Another main trait of these types of urban legends is that there is a moral message implied. In the one above, there is a feeling of powerlessness in the world, as if your destiny or fate is controlled from a higher power. Some people believe this, and they are probably the ones forwarding this email. For others, who believe that they alone control their own path in life, they probably just delete the email and forget about it.

Another trait that is common in most of these email urban legends is the threat of not acting. Not only will good things happen to you if you forward this email, but bad things will happen to you if you don't. Of course, the rewards and risks are always very vague (wishes coming true versus bad luck for years).

Beware The Greeks

WARNING! BEWARE GREEKS BEARING GIFTS!

If you receive a gift in the shape of a large wooden horse do not download it! It is extremely destructive and will overwrite your entire city!

The "gift" is disguised as a large wooden horse about two stories tall. It tends to show up outside the city gates and appears to be abandoned.

DO NOT let it through the gates! It contains hardware that is incompatible with Trojan programming, including a crowd of heavily armed Greek warriors that will destroy your army, sack your town, and kill your women and children. If you have already received such a gift, DO NOT OPEN IT! Take it back out of the city unopened and set fire to it by the beach.

FORWARD THIS MESSAGE TO EVERYONE YOU KNOW!

- Poseidon

~ ~ ~

This tongue-in-cheek email plays on the Greek mythology. The basic short version of the story is that in ancient times, the Greeks were at war with the Trojans. The Greeks sent a large wooden horse to the City of Troy as a gift. The Trojans were surprised and pleased that such a huge horse was presented as a gift, and they opened their fortress gates to the city and let in the wooden horse. Later that night, a secret door opened up and an army of Greek soldiers, now inside the city, attacked the Trojans and won the battle. There is a more in-depth article at http://darter.ocps.net/classroom/who/darter1/trhorse.htm if you are interested in reading more about the history of the Greeks and the Trojans.

There are computer viruses known as "Trojan Horses" that attack computers in the workplace and at home. The reason they are known as Trojan Horses is that they are disguised as something that you might enjoy downloading, such as a game or a screensaver. Once the program is inside your computer (or "inside your city walls") it waits for a little while and then attacks your computer system. Examples of damage include corrupting files, sending another Trojan Horse to everyone in your email address book, or even allowing a hacker to enter your computer and operate it by remote control.

While the above email is intended as a piece of humour, there is nothing funny about real Trojan Horse emails that may one day find themselves in your inbox. Be careful when opening up emails and running executable files on your computer.

Abraham Lincoln – John F. Kennedy Coincidences

Subject: Amazing Coincidences!

Check out these amazing coincidences between Abraham Lincoln and John F. Kennedy. Weird!

- Lincoln was elected in 1860, Kennedy in 1960, 100 years apart.
- Both men were deeply involved in civil rights for African Americans.
- Both men were assassinated on a Friday, in the presence of their wives.
- Each wife had lost a child while living at the White House.
- Both men were killed by a bullet that entered the head from behind.
- Lincoln was killed in Ford's Theatre. Kennedy met his death while riding in a Lincoln convertible made by the Ford Motor Company.
- Both men were succeeded by vice-presidents named Johnson who were southern Democrats and former senators.
- Andrew Johnson was born in 1808. Lyndon Johnson was born in 1908, exactly one hundred years later.
- The first name of Lincoln's private secretary was John, the last name of Kennedy's private secretary was Lincoln.
- John Wilkes Booth was born in 1839 [according to some sources] Lee Harvey Oswald was born in 1939, one hundred years later.
- Both assassins were Southerners who held extremist views.
- Both assassins were murdered before they could be brought to trial.
- Booth shot Lincoln in a theatre and fled to a warehouse. Oswald shot Kennedy from a warehouse and fled to a theatre.
- LINCOLN and KENNEDY each has 7 letters.

- ANDREW JOHNSON and LYNDON JOHNSON each has 13 letters.
- JOHN WILKES BOOTH and LEE HARVEY OSWALD each has 15 letters.
- A Lincoln staffer (named Miss Kennedy) told him not to go to the Theatre. A Kennedy staffer (named Miss Lincoln) told him not to go to Dallas.
- Abraham Lincoln was elected to Congress in 1846. John F. Kennedy was elected to Congress in 1946.
- Both assassins were known by their three names.

~ ~ ~

The simple fact of the matter is that people enjoy drawing similarities and conclusions to seemingly unrelated events. This is human nature. There does appear to be a number of coincidences surrounding these two presidents, and specific comments on some of them follow:

- *"Lincoln was elected in 1860, Kennedy in 1960, 100 years apart."*
While this is certainly interesting, it is by no means unfathomable. People just enjoy round numbers such as 100. Remember when your odometer in your car goes to 40,000? Everyone usually stares transfixed on the dial until it turns 40,001. This is more a comment on our human nature than in any unearthly, cosmic alignment. Also, remember that the U.S. Presidential elections are held every four years, so the chances of this happening drops from "1 in 100" down to "1 in 25" very quickly.

- *"Both men were deeply involved in civil rights for African Americans."*
This is not hugely surprising, considering that most U.S. presidents have been concerned with human rights, the rights of minorities, and the rights "of the working man." It is an interesting coincidence, however, that the two leaders were involved during the most intense periods in U.S. history concerning civil rights.

- *"Both men were assassinated on a Friday, in the presence of their wives."*
This is a rather interesting coincidence, it would seem. However, it appears that Lincoln was actually shot late Thursday (in the theatre) and died a few hours later on Friday. It is also interesting to note that both Presidents were

shot at public events. It would seem that if you wanted to assassinate an important political figure, the easiest way to get near them would be at a public event. And most of these events happen on or near the weekend.

• *"Each wife had lost a child while living at the White House."*
Back in Abraham Lincoln's day, illness and disease were more common than the conditions a century later. Edward "Eddie" Baker Lincoln was born in 1846 and died in 1850, due to a prolonged illness. Willie Lincoln was the third child of four and died in 1862 in the White House, at the young age of eleven. He died of Typhoid. Thomas Lincoln was the youngest son and died at the age of eighteen, in 1871. The oldest son, Robert Todd Lincoln, actually lived to the ripe old age of eighty-two. So, three of the four Lincoln children died at early ages, and one of those three were in the White House. As far as the JFK situation 100 years later, Jackie did suffer a stillbirth while in the White House. So, while the statement is true, once it is broken down and analyzed a bit further, the two facts don't seem so cosmically intertwined, as one died during birth and the other died as a child.

• *"Both men were killed by a bullet that entered the head from behind."*
This would seem to be the most logical place to shoot a public target, especially with the intent to assassinate. There is nothing particularly profound about this coincidence.

• *"Lincoln was killed in Ford's Theatre. Kennedy met his death while riding in a Lincoln convertible made by the Ford Motor Company."*
Now it would appear that we are just stretching for ties that bind. While this may be true, there is no apparent connection between a convertible and a theatre, other than the name.

• *"Both men were succeeded by vice-presidents named Johnson who were Southern Democrats and former senators."*
This one may appear fantastic on the surface, but if we follow it through, it would make sense. Since both Lincoln and JFK were from the North, it would seem reasonable to pick southern running mates. And by the time a politician has reached Presidential status, they have usually held some form of office such as governor or senator. How many Presidents and Vice Presidents have never held another office?

• *"John Wilkes Booth was born in 1839 [according to some sources] Lee Harvey Oswald was born in 1939, one hundred years later."*
Some people argue that John Wilkes Booth was born in 1838. So this coincidence, if true, is interesting, but loses some merit amidst the argument of the exact year of birth.

• *"Both assassins were known by their three names."*
It is interesting to note that this one is absolutely true. However, the assassins were only known this way *after* their crimes. Before, when they were "normal citizens," they were known only by their first and last names.

• *"Booth ran from the theatre and was caught in a warehouse. Oswald ran from a warehouse and was caught in a theatre."*
Well, this one is almost true. The Oswald part of the story is true, but Booth actually was apprehended in a barn. I guess that is a warehouse, technically speaking, but it is kind of a stretch.

• *"Booth and Oswald were assassinated before their trials."*
This is also true. However, the coincidence seems to end there. While Lee Harvey Oswald was arrested and then killed later, John Wilkes Booth was killed that very same night that he shot Lincoln. He was caught in the barn and shot by Federal agents.

The bottom line is that some people enjoy coincidences on a casual level, as a form of amusement, while others tend to think that there is more to it than simple chance.

Does the government know what race you are? What is the mystery behind the social security numbers?

Social Security Number Racial Code

Subject: Creepy Government

My grandfather has been doing research and discovered something that I was unaware of. He has discovered that the second middle number (the fifth number) in an African American's social security number is an even number while other nationalities have odd numbers.

This allows a person, organization, institution or whatever to claim that they are not discriminating against African Americans. However, they can tell our nationality simply by looking at our social security number and can, therefore, discriminate against us without us knowing.

You might want to do your own little research. What are your African American friends', relatives', and co-workers' middle numbers and what are your Caucasian friends' and co-workers' middle numbers? Maybe we can find out if this is the case on a larger scale. White people might really be getting over on us by making us feel like there is no way to discriminate against us if we don't put "African-American" or "black" on a school application, loan application or job application.

But if this secret race indicator is true, that's all they need to reject us. The more people you ask, the more valid the point will be. You might not want to tell anyone the real reason why you are asking until we can find out if this is true.

~ ~ ~

I could find no evidence to support this rumour. It would appear that the United States government basically hands out Social Insurance numbers in a

117

chronological order.

In Canada, I had asked a human resources professional if he had ever heard of this. He had heard once that there might be a "secret formula" used in Canada to determine if a Social Insurance Number (SIN) was valid. He said that he had heard that apparently you can add up the Canadian SIN numbers and apply them to some mathematical formula to determine if they had been forged or not. Unfortunately, he did not know what the specific formula was. I could also find no evidence of this formula, or anyone who had used such a formula. So far, the United States and Canadian governments appeared clean.

There are meanings behind some of the Social Security Numbers that the United States issues, but they are not related to race or ethnic background. The first three numbers indicate to authorities which state the citizen lived in at the time the card was issued. The second set of numbers pertains to the date that the card was issued.

I had also heard a rumour that there was a special SIN number in Canada for immigrants. The first number of their SIN was a "9". This way, employers could just read their SIN number to see if the applicant had been born in Canada, or just applied for citizenship. Was this yet another devious way for Canadian employers to discriminate? One of my friends is an immigrant, and her first number on her SIN is a six. She had never heard of such a thing. This one would appear to be false as well. I was zero for three.

It would appear that if there is a grand conspiracy of numbers, either with the Canadian SIN or with the American Social Security Numbers, it is not widely known. There are plenty of people online who are more than willing to voice up and claim that these "racially based" ID numbers is just a fallacy.

118

Think Before You Drink And Drive

On the last day before Christmas, I hurried to go to the supermarket to buy the last of my remaining gifts. When I saw all the people there, I started to complain to myself. It was going to take forever and I still had so many other places to go. Christmas really is getting more and more annoying every year.

Nonetheless, I made my way to the toy section. I started to curse the prices, wondering if kids really enjoy such expensive toys. While looking in the toy section, I noticed a small five-year old boy who was pressing a doll against his chest. He kept on touching the hair of the doll and looked so sad.

I wondered who the doll was for. The little boy turned to an old woman next to him: "Granny, are you sure I don't have enough money?"

The old lady replied, "You know that you don't have enough money to buy this doll, my dear." Then she asked him to stay there for five minutes while she went to look around. She left quickly. The little boy was still holding the doll in his hand. Finally, I started to walk towards him, and I asked him who he wanted to give this doll to. "It is the doll that my sister loved most. She really wanted it so much for Christmas. She was so sure that Santa Claus would bring it to her."

I replied to him that maybe Santa Claus will bring it to her after all, and not to worry. But he replied to me, "No, Santa Claus cannot bring it to her where she is now. I have to give the doll to my mother so that she can give it to her when she goes there. "

"My sister has gone to be with God. Daddy says that Mummy will also go to see God very soon, so I thought that she could take the doll with her to give to my sister." My heart nearly stopped. The little boy looked up at me and said, "I told Daddy to tell Mummy not to go yet. I asked him to wait until I came back from the supermarket." Then he showed me a very nice photo of him where he was laughing. He then told me, "I also want mummy to take this photo with her so that she will not forget me. I love my Mummy, and I wish she didn't have to leave me, but Daddy says that she has to go to be with my little sister."

I quickly reached for my wallet and took a few notes. I said to the boy, "What if we checked again, just in case if you have enough money?"

"OK," he said. "I hope that I have enough." I added some of my money to his without him seeing and we started to count it. There was enough for the doll and even some left over. The little boy said, "Thank you God for giving me enough money".

Then he looked at me and added, "I asked yesterday before I went to sleep for God to make sure I have enough money to buy this doll so that Mummy can give it to my sister. He heard me. I also wanted to have enough money to buy a white rose for my Mummy, but didn't dare to ask God for too much. But he gave me enough to buy the doll and the white rose. You know my mummy loves white roses".

A few minutes later, the old lady came back again. I finished my shopping in a totally different state from when I started. I couldn't get the little boy out of my mind. Then I remembered a local newspaper article.

Two days ago, the paper wrote about a drunk man in a truck who hit a car where there was one young lady and a little girl. The little girl died right away, and the mother was left in a critical state. The family had to decide whether to pull the plug on the life-assisting machine because the young lady would not be able to get out of the coma.

Was this the family of the little boy? Two days after this encounter with the little boy, I read in the newspaper that the young lady had passed away. I couldn't stop myself, and I went to buy a bunch of white roses. I went to the mortuary where the body of the young woman was exposed for people to see and make last wishes before burial. She was there, in her coffin, holding a beautiful white rose in her hand with the photo of the little boy and the doll placed over her chest. I left the place crying, feeling that my life had been changed forever. The love that this little boy had for his mother and his sister is still, to this day, hard to imagine. And in a fraction of a second, a drunk man had taken all this away from him.

Now you have 2 choices:

1) Send this message to everybody that you know.
2) Delete it and do as if it never touched your heart.

If you send this message, maybe you will help prevent someone drunk to go driving.

~ ~ ~

It doesn't really matter if this particular story is true or not. Drunk driving is a major killer in our society, and we should do more to promote its awareness. Even if the above story is completely made up, there are definitely cases where parents and loved ones were killed or horribly injured because of drunk drivers.

When the terrorist attacks of September 11th killed thousands of people in New York City, the news stations filled their time with photos, human-interest stories and non-stop reporting for weeks. However, drunk driving kills thousands per year, every year, and the average awareness just isn't very high. We shouldn't wait until its too late to appreciate our family and act responsibly.

The Dead Rabbit

My husband and I have lived at our current home for a couple of years now. This was our first home, and we had made a lot of effort to become friends with the neighbours. We had a dog, Max, who was one year old at the time. Recently, my husband came home and discovered our neighbours' pet rabbit, 'Puffy', firmly gripped between the jaws of our beloved pup. You can imagine the horror on my husband's face as he ordered our dog to let go. The rabbit, once a white ball of fluff, had turned into a limp ball of mud and blood.

In a fit of panic, my husband washed what was left of the bunny and fluffed it up with my hair dryer. Luckily, the neighbours were not home. They had gone to collect their children from school. My husband put the dead rabbit back in her hutch and sat down for a beer.

When my husband told me the story, I was certain that our neighbours would call our local council and have the dog put down. Around dinner time that evening we heard the children playing outside in their yard. Then, suddenly, one of the children let out a horrific scream. We could hear the kids crying, and we knew that they'd found the dead bunny in the hutch.

We avoided our neighbours for a couple of weeks. However, time passed and soon the incident made its way to the back of our minds. One weekend while watering the garden, my husband yelled hello to the neighbours across the fence. They walked over and had a casual chat. My husband casually asked about the screams he'd heard that evening a couple of weeks ago from the children.

"Oh yeah," said our neighbour in bewilderment. "It was the strangest thing. About a month ago the kids' bunny died. And then two weeks later it was back in the hutch, all washed and fluffed."

~ ~ ~

I enjoyed this one, although it has no doubt been passed around long before the advent of email. I was at a speaking engagement a number of years ago and heard the speaker tell this story, almost line for line. This story is a good example of how tall tales and urban legends sometimes just get transferred to the electronic medium, ensuring that incredibly old stories will live on.

The
Almighty
Dollar

$

Big Business Promotions

Hello everyone, and thank you for signing up for my Beta e-mail Tracking Application or BETA for short. My name is Bill Gates. Here at Microsoft we have just compiled an e-mail tracing program that tracks everyone to whom this message is forwarded to. It does this through a unique IP (internet protocol) address log book database.

We are experimenting with this and need your help. Forward this to everyone you know and if it reaches 1,000 people everyone on the list will receive $1,000 and a copy of Windows 98 at my expense.

Note: Duplicate entries will not be counted. You will be notified by e-mail with further instructions once this e-mail has reached 1,000 people. Windows 98 will not be shipped until it has been released to the general public.

Your friend,
Bill Gates & The Microsoft Development Team

~ ~ ~

There are many of these circulating around. They have been around for years, and no doubt they will continue to be among the most widely spreading of all the urban legends. After all, the only way for you to claim your reward is to pass it along. Virtually every one of these that you see are completely untrue. Here are a couple more that are similar.

Hello Disney fans,

And thank you for signing up for Bill Gates' BETA e-mail tracking. My name is Walt Disney Jr. Here at Disney we are working with Microsoft which has just compiled an e-mail tracing program that tracks everyone to whom this message is forwarded to. It does this through a unique IP (internet protocol) address log book database.

We are experimenting with this and need your help. Forward this to everyone you know and if it reaches 13,000 people, 1,300 of the people on the list will receive $5,000 and the rest will receive a free trip for two to Walt Disney World for one week during the summer at our expense. Enjoy.

Note: Duplicate entries will not be counted. You will be notified by e-mail with further instructions once this e-mail has reached 13,000 people.

Your friends,
Walt Disney Jr., Disney, Bill Gates & The Microsoft Development Team

~~~

Hello:
We here at the Miller Brewing Company, Inc. would like to help bring in the new year in style for everyone. We like to think of ourselves as a progressive company, keeping up with our customers. We have found that the best way to do this is through the internet and through e-mail.

We would like to make a special offer to our customers: If this e-mail makes it to 2,000,000 people by midnight on New Year's Eve 1999, we will send a coupon for one six-pack of any of our Miller Brand beverages.

In the event that 2,000,000 people are reached, our tracker / counter (embedded in this message) will report to us with the list of names and e-mail addresses. Thereafter, each e-mail address will be sent an electronic coupon which you can print out and redeem at any Miller

Brand beverage carrying store. The coupons will be sent as 2,000,000 people are reached, so the sooner, the better.

Enjoy, and cheers,

Miller Brewing Company, Inc.

~ ~ ~

There are countless "business giveaway" emails being forwarded around everyday. I presented three different promotional giveaways, so that you could see the similarities and differences in each one. The company or business may change, and the products being offered are often different, but basically the message is the same - send this e-mail along and you too can be the lucky recipient of a FREE item. I have seen M&M candies, free holidays, cellular phones, cash, clothing items, even whole computers, and other products being given away. You name it, and you can probably win it.

True or False? Of course, it is impossible to say that EVERY single one of these that you will ever see is false. It is impossible to say for certain that every e-mail you will ever receive is phoney promotion. However, the ones shown above are false. These companies have claimed that no such promotion exists. Often there is a phoney signature at the bottom. The Microsoft "tracking" system that these e-mails refer to does not exist at this time.

Be very wary before sending along "free items" e-mails. All you may be doing is annoying your co-workers and friends.

The Dying Boy

PLEASE READ THIS!! Here is your chance to make a difference in someone's life. There is a seven-year old boy named Greg Shergold. He has been diagnosed with a terminal brain tumour. He is in the hospital, slowly dying. He will never grow up to become a normal adult.

Greg's dream is to have his name in the Guinness Book of World Records. YOU can help him achieve his dream. He wants to hold the world record for receiving the most postcards.

~ ~ ~

Sometimes the e-mail will ask that you send business cards, or simply e-mail a "get well" response to another e-mail address. But in any event, you are helping a dying boy! Or are you?

I had received this e-mail, or a similar one to it, a few times over the last five years. Each time I was wary of spending my time and energy on a cause when I really had no proof that this was real.

I have discovered "spamming and urban legends" web pages that debunk such claims. Before you forward along a postcard, get well card, email, or especially money, please be sure to check the source. Does the email mention the name of the hospital (or even the city) where he or she is staying? Is there any proof that any of the claims are verifiable? Is there a phone number, or an email address of the hospital? While good intentions are honourable, sending a note to a non-existent person is a waste of your time.

How To Beat a Traffic Ticket

Subject: Beating A Traffic Ticket!
Just thought I would share this with you. I work in the ticket enforcement division, and in the course of my investigation into fines, their payment methods, and how points are assessed against drivers licenses, we discovered something very interesting if you get a traffic ticket.

This has been tried and it works ... if you ever get in this situation, you have an out.

We discovered that this procedure works in every state. Read it and try it, for you have nothing to lose but the points on your license. This is how it works.

If you get a speeding ticket, or a ticket for going through a red light or whatever the case may be, and you are going to get points deducted off your license, then there is a method to ensure that you DO NOT get any points taken off.

The trick is this - when you get your fine, send in the check to pay for it. But, make sure to overpay the fine. For example, if the fine is $79, then make the check out for $82, or some other small amount over the fine. The computer system will then have to send you back a check for the difference, but here is the trick!

DO NOT CASH THE REFUND CHECK!

Throw the check away! Here's how it works - points are not assessed to your license until all financial transactions are complete. If you do not cash the check, then all of the transactions are NOT complete. However, the computer system has gotten its money will not bother you any more.

This information came to our attention from a very reliable computer company that sets up the standard database used by each state's Department of Motor Vehicles. Good luck - and share this with all your friends!

~ ~ ~

This one sounds too great to be true, and it most likely is. If there were any seeds of truth in this one, it might have once revolved around a computer glitch or error in one Department of Motor Vehicles in some industrialized country, but it is hard to imagine a serious flaw such as this finding itself in every computer in every motor vehicles office in the United States.

If you have violated the law, and pay the fine, then you have essentially admitted your guilt. If you dispute the charge, the guilt or innocence is determined in traffic court, not in the computer system. That is also where the points are subtracted.

Pretty far-fetched, but most people would assume that there's "no harm done" in passing along great advice. After all, what do you have to lose? Probably nothing, except the refund cheque that you are ripping up and throwing in the garbage.

In my research on this urban legend, I came across reports that indicate that this rumour originated in Australia in 1998. However, there was no detail provided to indicate that the debunkers were any more legitimate than the actual rumours. It is interesting to read various posting sites where urban legends are discussed. Although the majority of them are not well written, there are often some good points raised, where people try to logically reason their way through these and other legends. However, many people just say things like "it's not true, it was a rumour that started five years ago in Asia." They don't provide any research documentation, such as the sources that brought them to that particular conclusion. In effect, their "explanation" of the urban legend is no more valid than the very tale that they are trying to criticize.

The Hunger Site - To Good to be True?

FW: UN Hunger Site
The Hunger Site is a wonderful website. All you do is click a button and somewhere in the world some hungry person gets a meal to eat - at NO cost to you. The food is paid for by corporate sponsors. All you do is go to the site and click. But, you're only allowed one click per day, so spread the word to others.

Visit the site and pass the word!
http://www.thehungersite.com

~ ~ ~

The Hunger Site is definitely a real website. But can you really help people out without spending any of your own money?

The answer is yes. And the reason for this is advertising. The website is sponsored by companies who have their ads on the page. When you click on The Hunger Site's "Give Free Food" button, you are transported to the sponsor's page, where you can view the day's sponsors. Based on the number of sponsors, your click donates a certain amount of "staple food" to a hungry child somewhere in the world. The Hunger Site encourages you to do business with these socially conscious companies.

There are other, related sites from The Hunger Site that work in a similar fashion. They are:

- Breast Cancer Site - fund free mammograms
- Child Health Site - prevent life-threatening diseases in children
- Rainforest Site - preserve land in the rainforest
- Animal Rescue Site - provide food for an animal in need

You can also order clothing, gifts and jewellery from these sites, and a portion of the proceeds help support the different causes. We can all be happy that this urban legend is true.

Chain Letter - Get Rich Quick!

Subject: It Works. Its Legal. Its Easy. So Why Not?
WOMAN FINDS $71,000 IN SON'S CLOSET
Does this headline look familiar? Of course it does.

You most likely have just seen this story recently featured on a major nightly news program in the United States.

The mother was putting laundry away when she came across a large brown paper bag that was suspiciously buried beneath some clothes and a skateboard in the back of her 15-year-old son's closet. Nothing could have prepared her for the shock she got when she opened the bag and found it was full of cash. Five dollar bills, twenties, fifties and hundreds - all neatly rubber-banded in labelled piles.

"My first thought was that he had robbed a bank", says the 41-year-old woman, "There was over $71,000 dollars in that bag - that's more than my husband earns in a year".

The woman immediately called her husband at the car dealership where he worked to tell him what she had discovered. He came home right away and they drove together to the boy's school and picked him up. Little did they suspect that where the money came from was more shocking than actually finding it in the closet.

As it turns out, the boy had been sending out a type of 'chain-letter' to email addresses that he obtained off of the Internet. Every day after school for the past three months, he had been doing this right on his computer in his bedroom.

"I just got the email one day and I figured I would put my name on it like the instructions said and I started sending it out," said the clever 15-year-old.

The email chain letter listed 3 addresses and contained instructions to send one $5 dollar bill to the person at the top of the list, then delete that address and move the other 2 addresses up, and finally to add your name to the bottom of the list. The letter went on to state that you would receive "several thousand dollars in five dollar bills" within 2 weeks if you sent out the letter with your name at the bottom of the 3-address list. "I didn't think it was gonna work," the boy continued.

Within the first few days of sending out the email, the PO box that his parents had gotten him for his video-game magazine subscriptions began to fill up with envelopes containing $5 dollar bills.

"About a week later I rode my bike down to the post office and my box had 1 magazine and about 300 envelopes stuffed in it. There was also a yellow slip that said I had to go up to the post office counter. I thought I was in trouble or something. I went up to the counter and they had another whole box of mail for me. I had to ride back home and empty out my backpack 'cause I couldn't carry it all," he exclaimed.

Over the next few weeks, the boy continued sending out the email. "The money just kept coming in and I just kept sorting it and stashing it in the closet. I barely had time for my homework." He had also been riding his bike to several of the area's banks and exchanging the $5 bills for twenties, fifties and hundreds.

"I didn't want the banks to get suspicious, so I kept going to different banks with about five to ten thousand at a time in my backpack. I would usually tell the lady at the bank counter that my dad had sent me in to exchange the money and he was outside waiting for me. One time the lady gave me a really strange look and told me that she wouldn't be able to do it for me, and that my dad would have to come in and do it. But I just rode to the next bank down the street," he laughed.

"Surprisingly, the boy didn't have any reason to be afraid. The reporting news team examined and investigated the so-called 'chain-letter' the boy was sending out and found that it wasn't a chain-letter at all. In fact, it was completely legal according to:

-US Postal and Lottery Laws, Title 18, Section 1302 and 1341

Title 18, Section 3005 in the US code

Code of federal regulations, Volume 16, Sections 255 and 436

which state that a product or service must be exchanged for money received. Every five dollar bill that he received contained a little note that read, "Please add me to your mailing list". This simple note made the letter legal because he was exchanging a service (adding the purchaser's name to his mailing list) for a five dollar fee.

Here is the letter that the 15-year-old was sending out by email. You can do the exact same thing he was doing, simply by following the instructions in this letter.

Here are instructions on how to make $10,000 US cash in the next 2 weeks:

There are 3 addresses listed below.

Send the person at the top of the list a $5 bill wrapped in 2 pieces of paper (to securely hide it), along with a note that says: "Please add me to your mailing list".

Then delete that name, move the other 2 up and put your name at the bottom.

Now start sending this ENTIRE e-mail back out to people.

When 20 people receive it, those 20 people will move your name up to the middle position and they will each send out 20. That totals 400 people that will receive this letter with your name in the middle.

Then, those 400 people will move your name up to the top and they will each send out 20 E-mails. That totals 8,000 people that will receive this E-mail with your name at the top and they will each send you a $5 bill.

$8,000 people each sending you a $5 bill = $40,000 cash. That's if everyone responds to this E-mail, but not everyone will, so you can expect more realistically to receive about $10,000 in cash ($5 bills) in your mailbox.

This will work for anyone, anywhere in the world in any country, but send only a US CASH $5 bill.

The more E-mails you send out, the more cash you will receive. If

each person sends out 100 E-mails, there will be 1,000,000 people that receive this letter when your name reaches the top. If only 1% of those peoplerespond, you will still get $50,000 cash.
Here is the list:

1 - T. Nolley
xxxxx Club Cir.
Indianapolis, IN 46229

2 - Leonard E. Hawkins
xxxx Cooley RD.
Winter Have, FL 33880

3 - William Watner
xxxx Montello DR.
Orlando, FL 32817

THERE'S NOTHING MORE TO DO. When your name reaches the top in a few days, you will start receiving $5 bills from other people just like yourself, who are willing to invest a $5 bill to receive $10,000 cash.
If you don't try it - you will never know.

~ ~ ~

The age-old multi-level mailing program - the chain letter - is a favourite source of spam on the web. Now people have discovered the power of urban myths to spread their viral marketing campaign even further. This one is wrapped in a mythical news story that describes the incredible tale of a 15 year old kid who amasses a fortune in his bedroom in his spare time by e-mailing chain letters. The young boy gets rich, and his mom discovers the stash hidden beneath dirty laundry and a skateboard.

The story serves a dual purpose: 1) it gets the reader interested through a human-interest angle, and 2) it explains how this form of chain letter is actually "legal", since the money you send has a note saying "Please add me to your mailing list," which the story claims makes it OK since now a "service" is being exchanged. We're sure the Postal Police would disagree.

The chain letter is one of the oldest "get rich quick" schemes and for a few, it actually does work. The chain letter is also related to the "envelope stuffing" scheme that you may have seen advertised as well. For example a newspaper may have a small classified ad like this:

"Make $1,000 a week stuffing envelopes! Find out how! Send $2 and self-addressed, stamped envelope to P.O. Box 1060, Anytown, U.S.A. "

Millions of people have fallen for this, and have sent in $2 to the advertiser, only to find that the envelopes that they are stuffing are the very self-addressed, stamped envelopes that you are sending in. The "advice" or "service" that the advertiser is providing to you is this:

"To make money, advertise in a newspaper exactly as I have done. People from around the world will send you $2, and you just send them back these very instructions. "

And the cycle continues. This money-making scheme is not perfect; in fact their are two large flaws in the logic of the envelope stuffer or the chain letter. It assumes that everyone (or a significant portion, or any portion) of people will send you money. This just isn't the case. The other, and stronger argument, is that there are only a finite number of people on the planet. Eventually, after the chain letter has changed hands on a number of times, you just run out of people that you can send the letter to. For example, in the email, the claim is made that 1,000,000 people will be reached. Who are these people? Are they just sitting around, waiting to get rich? Unlikely. And if only 250 different people were to start off this email, within days, according to the logic, the email would reach 250 million people. However, there are only 250 million people in the entire United States, and not everyone has email. So, the logic starts to wear thin after close scrutiny.

Fed Ex *This*

Subject: Inspirational Story
Fred Smith, the founder of Federal Express, was attending Yale and had an assignment to write a business plan. Fred wrote up his idea for an overnight delivery service. The concept was based on a simple idea; crate a central hub where all packages would pass through during the day and be funnelled out overnight. The idea was to simplify the logistics of routing packages, and create a huge cost savings by centralizing operations.

Fred submitted his paper and was awarded a C.

Moral: Those who can, do. Those who can't, teach. Those who can't teach, teach at Yale.

~ ~ ~

This story would appear to be based on fact. In the book *Overnight Success: Federal Express & Frederick Smith, It's Renegade Creator* it would appear that the basic facts of the story are true. Professor Challas A. Hall Jr. marked the economics paper a "C".

In all fairness to the professor, even if the business plan had been the greatest and most innovative idea of the 20th century, it still might have been a poorly written paper. It is also interesting to note that there have been many wonderful and profound innovations in universities and colleges that have proved to be disasters in the business world. But it is interesting to look back on success stories and see the adversity that many of the influential people of our times have faced.

Post Its

A 3M researcher, Spencer Silver, was attempting to invent a super-adhesive. One of the batches he created was a flop, so he set it aside in the lab to work on another batch.

Later, another researcher remembered the substance when he was annoyed with bookmarks that kept falling out of his hymnal. He started applying this substance to his bookmarks. He was so pleased that he began showing this little invention around the office. He pointed this out to Spencer, who realized he had invented quite accidentally an "unglue".

The marketing department at 3M refused to believe the product would work, so Fry put together a bunch of samples and sent them to secretaries around the office. They loved the product. Upper management got wind of the invention, and the Post It was born. Spencer and Fry were given $500 for their invention, which produces $300 million in sales annually.

Moral: Turn lemons into lemonade. And keep the profits.

~ ~ ~

Again, the basic elements of the story appear to be true. However, in the book "In Search of Excellence" by Tom Peters, it would appear that 3M management did in fact try to market the product (as opposed to refusing "to believe the product would work"). Instead of sending samples to the secretaries in the office, 3M sent samples to secretaries of Fortune 500 companies. Essentially the story is accurate, however.

The Mexican Chevy Nova

GM began shipping the Chevy Nova to Mexico in the late 60s. Thousands of Novas were sent south of the border, but sales were poor, and the home office wanted to know why. Was it performance? Price? Poor advertising and PR? Was the pre-NAFTA Mexican government somehow to blame?.

GM sent a busload of executives down to Mexico to investigate. The Nova had sold well in the US, was priced right for the market, and the marketing mix looked about right. So how come no one in Mexico was buying? A young enterprising manager suggested a focus group, which was quickly put together. Twelve professional, well-educated Mexicans were shown the commercials, product brochures and other materials, and asked if they would buy the car. A few started laughing, and said of course, no. The moderator asked why not? Price? Performance? "No, not that," said one member of the focus group. "Why should we buy a car that doesn't go?"

The moderator immediately understood, got up and excused himself to the back room, where the GM executives were sipping Tecates and eating tamales. "Nobody will buy your car!" He said.

"Why not?" asked the head of marketing.

"Simple. Because the name Nova in Spanish means, "It Doesn't go".

Moral: If it no go, then I no buy.

~ ~ ~

This story sounds great. It shows that big business, with their fancy executives and high-priced marketing gurus, would overlook such a simple and huge error. It makes Chevy out to be confused and befuddled.

In fact Nova in Mexican does translate into "No Go", but this apparently did not deter sales of the Chevy Nova. The vehicle has sold well in Mexico. It is unlikely that Mexican citizens would take the name of a foreign car so literally, especially if the price was right and it was a quality automobile.

The Classic Coke Myth

Subject: Check the Coke Can!!
A man in Central Park, New York, purchased a bottle of Coke and a hot dog. The man gulped down the hot dog and then turned his attention to the bottle of cold soda.

About a few gulps the man realized something was wrong with his Coke. When he looked into the bottle, he noticed that there was a strange object inside. He poured out the contents of the bottle into the nearby sewer drain and looked into the bottle. There was a dead rat inside.

The poor man immediately became sick, had a seizure and, before the ambulances arrived, died of a heart attack.

~ ~ ~

Of course, the biggest objection that immediately surfaces is "how could a rat possibly stick its body into a skinny Coke bottle?" Sometimes the story features a mouse instead, and sometimes it is a Coke can instead of a bottle. But, as you can imagine, this very general urban legend has been around for literally decades. There is no evidence to support that any of this story is true. If it, or anything even remotely like it had ever occurred, it would have been many years ago, because this urban legend has been around since before the inception of the internet. This is one of the all-time most popular urban legends, and you will no doubt come across a story like it during your lifetime. The details will change, but one thing won't: people seem to enjoy telling each other about horrid objects in food and beverage.

144

Procter & Gamble Are Involved With...The Devil?

Subject: Make a difference in the world!

The President of Procter & Gamble appeared on the *Sally Jesse Raphael Show* on March 1, 1998. He announced that, "due to the openness of our society," he was coming out of the closet about his association with the Church of Satan. He stated that a large portion of his profits from Procter & Gamble Products goes to support The Church of Satan!

Sally Jesse asked whether or not stating his associations on television would hurt his business. He replied, "There are not enough Christians in the United States to make a difference."

The P & G product list includes the following.

Cleaning supplies: Bold, Cascade, Cheer, Comet, Ivory Dreft, Joy, Dash, Oxidol, Spic & Span, Tide, Top Job, Gain, Mr. Clean, Lest Oil, Bounty Towels

Food: Duncan Hines, Dehydrated Fruits, Fisher Nuts, Fisher Mints,

Coffee: High Point, Folgers

Shortening Oils: Crisco, Puritan, Fluffo

Deodorants: Secret, Sure

Diapers: Pampers, Luvs

Hair Care: Head & Shoulders, Prell, Pert, Vidal Sassoon, Ivory, Pantene

Acne Product: Clearasil

Mouthwash/Toothpaste: Scope, Crest, Gleem

Peanut Butter: JIF

Personal Hygiene: Always, Attend Undergarments
Lotions: Oil of Olay, Wondra
Soap: Camay, Coast, Ivory, Lava, Safeguard, Zest, Oil of Olay
Fabric Softener: Downy, Bounce
Citrus Punch: Sunny Delight
Medication: Aleve, Pepto-Bismol

Look for Procter & Gamble's name written on the products, or the symbol of a ram's horn, which will appear on each product beginning on January 1, 2000.

The ram's horn will form the 666, also known as the number of the beast, or Satan's number.

You should remember that if you purchase any of these products, YOU will be contributing to the church of Satan.

Inform other Christians about this and STOP buying Procter & Gamble Products. Let's show Procter & Gamble that there are enough Christians to make a difference.

On a previous *Jenny Jones Show*, the owner of Procter &Gamble said that if Satan would prosper he would give his heart and soul to him. Then he gave Satan credit for his riches.

Anyone interested seeing this tape should send $3.00 to:

SALLY TRANSCRIPTS
515 WEST 57TH STREET
NEW YORK NY 10019

We urge you to make copies of this and pass it on to as many people as possible. This needs to stop. Liz Clayborne also professes to worship Satan and recently openly admitted on the Oprah Winfrey show that half of her profits go towards the church of Satan.

Procter & Gamble currently uses a corporate logo with Satanic connections. The logo is a drawing of the man in the moon, which contains 13 stars. This is a symbol of devil worship. And, if you look closely at the beard, the mark of the beast (666) can be seen in the hair lines.

~ ~ ~

Could it be that one of the largest companies in North America is run by a devil worshipper? And this happened not only on the *Sally Jesse Raphael Show*, but also on the *Jenny Jones Show* and *Oprah Winfrey Show* as well?

No. This is a great example of an email that is unbelievably fantastic, yet there is something about it that makes the reader want to believe that the story could be true. The specific sources given in the email make it seem credible at first, but basically the information given is completely false. The printed word appears to be factual, and has been for generations. There is something about seeing an email, in type, that somehow renders it more legitimate than if the story is simply told at a party. "But it must be true – I saw it in the newspaper! (Or television! Or in a book/magazine!" is a classic phrase that has been repeated over and over again throughout modern history.

There is definitely some truth to the saying "the more fantastic the lie, the more people will believe it."

Netscape and AOL's e-mail Tracker

Subject: Big Money?
A week ago I got an email from Microsoft asking me for my address. I gave it to them and yesterday I got a check in the mail for $800. It really works! I wanted you to get a piece of the action. You won't regret it.
Stan

FW:
Dear e-mail recipient,
Netscape and AOL have recently merged to form the largest internet company in the world. In an effort to remain at pace with this giant, Microsoft has introduced a new email tracking system as a way to keep Internet Explorer as the most popular browser on the market.

This email is a beta test of the new software and Microsoft has generously offered to compensate those who participate in the testing process. For each person you send this email to, you will be given $5. For every person they give it to, you will be given an additional $3. For every person they send it to you will receive $1.

Microsoft will tally all the emails produced under your name over a two week period and then email you with more instructions. This beta test is only for Microsoft Windows users because the email tracking device that contacts Microsoft is embedded into the code of Windows 95 and 98.

Get Free Email and Do More On The Web. Visit http://www.msn.com

~ ~ ~

This email best represents the stark greed that drives people to forward these messages. Imagine raking in hundreds of dollars, all for just forwarding around emails to your friends (or strangers, for that matter). But this simply isn't the case. It's just plain false.

E-mail Tax

Dear Internet Subscriber:

Please read the following carefully if you intend to stay online and continue using e-mail.

The last few months have revealed an alarming trend in the Government of the United States attempting to quietly push through legislation that will affect your use of the Internet. Under proposed legislation (Bill 602P) the U.S. Postal service will be attempting to bilk email users out of "alternative postage fees." Bill 602P will permit the Federal Govt. to charge 5 cents surcharge on every email delivered, by billing Internet Service Providers at source. The consumer would then be billed in turn by the ISP.

Washington D.C. lawyer Richard Stepp is working without pay to prevent this legislation from becoming law. The U.S. Postal Service is claiming that lost revenue due to the proliferation of email is costing nearly $230,000,000 in revenue per year. You may have noticed the recent ad campaign "There is nothing like a letter".

Since the average citizen received about 10 pieces of email per day in 1998, the cost to the typical individual would be an additional 50 cents per day, or over $180 per year, above and beyond their regular Internet costs. Note that this would be money paid directly to the U.S. Postal Service for a service they do not even provide.

The whole point of the Internet is democracy and non-interference. If the Federal Govt. is permitted to tamper with our liberties by adding a surcharge to e-mail, who knows where it will end?

You are already paying an exorbitant price for snail mail because of bureaucratic inefficiency. It currently takes up to 6 days for a letter to be delivered from New York to Buffalo. If the U.S. Postal Service is allowed to tinker with email, it will mark the end of the 'free' Internet in the United States. One congressman, Tony Schnell (R) has even suggested a "twenty to forty dollar per month surcharge on all Internet service" above and beyond the government's proposed email charges.

Note that most of the major newspapers have ignored the story, the only exception being the Washingtonian which called the idea of email surcharge "a useful concept whose time has come" (March 6th 1999 Editorial).

Don't sit by and watch your freedoms erode away! Send this email to all Americans on your list and tell your friends and relatives to write their congressman and say "No!" to Bill 602P.

Kate Turner, assistant to Richard Stepp Berger
Stepp and Gorman Attorneys at Law
216 Concorde Street, Vienna, VA.

~ ~ ~

This email certainly claims some serious happenings in the United States government. However, after a little digging, the details appear to be completely erroneous.

This posting is from the very informative web-page of the U.S. House of Representatives Web Page (www.house.gov):

SESSIONS DISPELS RUMORS OF E-MAIL TAX

(WASHINGTON) - U.S. Congressman Pete Sessions (R-Dallas) today dispelled a rumour claiming that a "Congressman Schnell" has introduced "Bill 602P," allowing the federal government to impose a 5-cent surcharge on all email messages sent over the Internet with revenue sent to the U.S. Postal Service (USPS). The erroneous charge has been circulating through a chain e-mail for the last several months.

"I have confirmed with the USPS that this email rumour is completely false," said Sessions. "There is no such Congressman in the U.S. House of Representatives, and bills are not named in this fashion. Furthermore, the USPS is not allowed to accrue revenue from non-postal sources."

I also logged on to *The Washingtonian* website at: www.washingtonian.com, who had this to say:

The message that is apparently out over the Internet about an "editorial" by The Washingtonian supporting an e-mail tax is a hoax.

We never wrote such an article or editorial. We do not have a "March 6" issue—we are a monthly magazine.

We at The Washingtonian do not know who started this rumour, but it is not true. The e-mail tax is a hoax.

Exam Scam

Subject: Exams

Two university students decided to go skiing for the weekend. They were having such a good time that they decided to skip the calculus exam that was scheduled for Monday morning. They wanted to get some final runs in before they headed back to school.

They decided to tell the calculus professor that they got a flat tire and therefore deserved to take the exam at a later, rescheduled time. Hearing the story, the calculus professor agreed that it really was just bad luck. He agreed that they could take the exam a later date.

A couple of weeks later, the professor greeted the two guys and placed them in two separate rooms to take the exam.

The first few questions were worth a minor 10% of the overall grade, and were quite easy. Both of them grew more confident as they finished the first section, positive that they had gotten away with fooling the professor. Then they turned to the second page.

The only question on the second page, worth 90% of the exam, was:

"Which tire?"

Time's Up

FW: Good Advice for Students!

A university student is having a very hard time writing a final exam. So hard, in fact, that he continues to write a full five minutes after the professor has called "Pencils down." The professor, tired of waiting, picks up the pile of exams and begins to walk out of the room.

Seeing this, the student finishes up and rushes, paper in hand, to the professor, only to find that his exam will not be accepted.

After the professor explains to the distraught student that he has violated academic code by writing past the finishing time, the student asks him: "Do you have any idea who I am?"

The professor answers, "No. But I'll have a pretty good idea what your name is when I record your failing grade."

With that, the student knocks the finished exams out of the professors hands, mixes his in with the pile, and runs out of the room.

Rumour has it, he got a B+.

Hotmail is Shutting Down

Fwd: Hotmail is shutting down, please read this if you have Hotmail.
Dear Hotmail User,
Because of the sudden rush of people signing up to Hotmail, it has come to our attention that we are vastly running out of resources. So, within a month's time, anyone who does not receive this email with the exact subject heading, will be deleted off our server. Please forward this email so that we know you are still using this account.
WARNING WARNING
Hotmail is overloading and we need to get rid of some people and we want to find out which users are actually using their Hotmail accounts. So if you are using your account, please pass this e-mail to every Hotmail user that you can and if you do not pass this letter to anyone we will delete your account.
From Mr. Jon Henerd
Hotmail Admin. Dept.

~ ~ ~

I find this email humorous because it is so poorly written. All of the details of a classic urban legend are there: the email is vague ("within a month's time") and the request to forward the email is there, as it is in so many cases.

I find it a little odd that an internet business such as Hotmail would suffer from the problem of "too many customers". How many e-commerce businesses would love to have that dilemma! Notice how Hotmail doesn't thank its customers for signing up, or even make mention of the customer's wishes or desires.

The other interesting point to note is that since Hotmail is a web-based email program, users need to log in to www.hotmail.com in order to use their accounts. So couldn't the people at Hotmail just check their logs for user activity? And it would stand to reason that if Hotmail was suffering from overloaded servers, then why would they request that you, the user, forward this email around to other people? Wouldn't that just clog up the servers even more? And why should you forward the email to another Hotmail user? Wouldn't they also have received the same email that you just did? It just doesn't make sense, and ranks up there as one of the poorer hoaxes floating around.

Anti-Semitism and Amazon.com

Dear Friends,

As you may know, *The Protocols of the Elders of Zion* was an anti-Semitic book written by the Czarist secret service early in this century, that has been supremely and fatally successful in spreading the theory of an international Jewish conspiracy to take over the world and harm non-Jews.

It is today a best seller among neo-Nazis, and in such countries as Jordan, Syria, Egypt and among the Palestinians. Experts on anti-Semitism see it as one of the most dangerous books ever written, responsible for the loss of untold Jewish lives.

Amazon.com has chosen to sell this book. That is their right, although legitimate booksellers in America do not sell it.

What is absolutely immoral and irresponsible, is that they review the book positively, saying that it has not been proven to be a "hoax" - that is, that it can be read as a valid expose of the Jewish plot to destroy everyone else.

The president of Amazon was informed about this problem, and nothing has been done to remove the review.

I would not shop in a store that sells neo-Nazi hate literature. I will let them know why.

P.S. please forward this letter to everyone on your email list. It is vitally important that Amazon.com realize that the American public will not support pandering to neo-Nazis for profit.

~ ~ ~

This urban legend is absolutely false. Amazon.com does indeed sell this book, as they are one of the largest book stores in the world. But did they positively review the book, and agree with the writings? The answer is no.

Check out http://www.amazon.com and just search for the title of the book. In fact, Amazon does write a review of this book, but they are not at all positive about the writings and is quick to point out the evil inherent in this book.

Some people may disagree with Amazon (or any bookseller) selling this book. There has always been the debate over free speech versus hateful propaganda. But it is not fair to accuse Amazon.com of favouring this book, because that is simply not the case.

Free Coca-Cola For a Month

Subject: FREE COKE! .

Coca-Cola is offering four free cases of diet coke or regular coke to every person you send this to. When you have finished sending this e-mail to as many people as you wish, a screen will come up. It will then ask where you want your free coke products sent. This is a sales promotion to get our name out to young people around the world.

We believe this project can be a success, but only with your help. So please start e-mailing and help us build our database. Thank you for your support!

Always Coca-Cola,
Mike Hill
Director of Marketing
Coca-Cola Corporation
Atlanta, Georgia

~ ~ ~

Here we go again with the email tracker. This apparently is a real concern for many internet and email users, because it has appeared in so many urban legends and emails. However, tracking email at this time is not a possibility. It is also interesting to note the vagueness in the email. By sending an email "to as many people as you want", you could, in theory, just send it to one person and you would start receiving free goods. It doesn't sound like a very sensible business practice. How much would shipping millions of cases of

Coke, all around the globe, cost the company?

At least Coca-Cola can feel like they are not alone. There are literally dozens of companies that have been targeted in these "free product" emails.

Anna Cohen Letter

Dear Friends,

My name is Anna Cohen and I live in Albany New York. My daughter Liz recently had a baby girl named Jada 2 months early. Jada has many problems with her heart and lungs and medical costs have become extremely expensive. Jada was recently moved to a hospital in California and the move was very expensive.

A billionaire in California has promised to give $.05 for every time this email is forwarded. If you wouldn't mind forwarding this to everyone on your list, I would greatly appreciate it, as well as my daughter and little Jada. This could save a life. Please have a heart and forward this.

Remember: What goes around comes around.

Thank you,

Anna Cohen

~ ~ ~

It is amazing that people would forward this email. It just doesn't make any sense if one follows it through logically. Of course there is the email tracking impossibility, but some people could ignore that. So let's assume for a minute that the email tracking technology did in fact exist. Why would a billionaire give out money based on the number of emails that were forwarded? If the billionaire was in charge of a big company, maybe there would be some advertising in the email. Or even the billionaire's name.

But there is no such information. By forwarding the email, you are not in any way helping out the billionaire. So if that is the case, why wouldn't the rich billionaire just give the needy family the money?

The best part of the email is the last part. "What goes around comes around." It is not enough to try to tug on your heartstrings; you receive an ominous threat as well.

Febreze Warning

FW: WARNING!

From the Veterinary Emergency Center in Needham, MA.:

Febreze, a new product that is used to get odours out of fabrics, has been causing deaths and illness in dogs, cats and birds. There have been multiple instances reported in the past few weeks of dogs, cats and birds dying after Febreze was used anywhere near them. Some dogs have only gotten very ill, but some have died. Several birds have died as well.

Febreze contains zinc chloride, which is the culprit. If you have recently sprayed your dog's bed with this product, please wash it until you get all of the Febreze out, or get your dog or cat new bedding. Please pass the word along to your friends so we can prevent further deaths.

~ ~ ~

Yet another warning about consumer products that simply is not true. At the ASPCA's website, found at http://www.aspca.org, the organization announced that they consider Febreze safe for pets when used as directed. The ASPCA does not know of any case where a dog or cat has died from exposure to Febreze.

On Febreze's own website (http://www.febreze.com) there is a "frequently asked question" (FAQ) link. The company says that Febreze is safe to use around pets, although they do caution that pet owner's should not spray the pets directly with Febreze.

Febreze speaks more directly to the internet urban legend in their "rumours" section of their website. Febreze says that scientists, safety experts and veterinarians have tested and used Febreze for five years and found it safe for use around pets. They do, however, mention that birds are "uniquely sensitive to some airborne household products" and that you should remove the bird from the room when spraying Febreze (or any other household cleaning product).

Tommy Hilfiger Rumour

Subject: Tommy Hilfiger

I'm sure many of you watched the recent taping of the Oprah Winfrey show where her guest was Tommy Hilfiger. On the show, she asked him if the statements about race he was accused of saying were true.

Statements like: "...If I'd known African-Americans, Hispanics, Jews and Asians would buy my clothes, I would not have made them so nice. I wish these people would NOT buy my clothes, as they are made for upper class white people."

His answer to Oprah was a simple "YES." Oprah then immediately asked him to leave her show.

Let's give him what he asked for. Let's not buy his clothes! Let's put him in a financial state where he himself will not be able to afford the ridiculous prices he puts on his clothes.

PLEASE SEND THIS MESSAGE TO ANYONE YOU KNOW WHO SPENDS THEIR HARD EARNED MONEY ON CLOTHES MADE BY SOMEONE WHO DOES NOT RESPECT THEM AS A PERSON OR A PEOPLE!

~ ~ ~

I could not find one credible source that substantiated this rumour. According to the above email, Tommy Hilfiger had appeared on the *Oprah Winfrey Show*. But no one seems to know what date this might have happened. However, there is another version of this rumour that has Tommy Hilfiger appearing on CNN. In both versions, Tommy Hilfiger makes racist comments and is thrown off of the show.

This is just not true. Note the lack of details in the above email. *When* did this happen? This was a supposed "recent" taping of Oprah Winfrey. Yet this email has been circulating for *years*.

Fight Back Against Gas Prices!

Subject: Fight Back!

It's time we did something about the price of gasoline in America! We are all sick and tired of high prices when there are literally millions of gallons of gasoline in storage.

You know what I found out? If there was just ONE day when no one purchased any gasoline, prices would drop drastically.

The so-called oil cartel has decided to slow production by some 2 million barrels per day to drive up the price. I have decided to see how many Americans we can get to NOT BUY ANY GASOLINE on one particular day!

Let's have a GAS OUT! Do not buy any gasoline on NOVEMBER 1, 2002 !!!!! Buy gas on the Thursday before, or the Saturday after. Do not buy any gasoline on FRIDAY, NOVEMBER 1, 2002.

Wanna help? Send this message to everyone you know. Ask them to do the same. All we need is a few million to participate in order to make a difference. Let me know how many you will send out. We CAN make a difference.

~ ~ ~

Every year it seems that consumers are frustrated at the rising price of certain necessities, such as groceries, clothing and, of course, gasoline. This email has been circulating for years, and each time the date changes. But can boycotting gasoline for one day really make a difference?

Unfortunately, the answer is most likely "no." We must keep in mind that most retail gas stores have no say in what their gas prices are. While it is true that consumers can affect the price of gasoline, there are only two ways to reasonably do it. The first is to purchase less gasoline overall. This would mean either travelling less, or using alternate means of transportation. The second way is to price compare when shopping.

Online, there is http:www.gasticker.com, which is a website designed for consumers to monitor gas prices in Canada. You can compare the price of gasoline in your region and then purchase gasoline where you like.

But wouldn't a day-long boycott of gasoline result in the price of gas falling sharply, as stores try to get rid of their inventory? One would think that this would be the case, but it just isn't true. In theory, if every single person in your local region did not buy gas for 24 hours, what would be the result? Firstly, your local merchant would suffer, as their daily sales would be quite low. They can't pay the rent on gum sales. But is your local retail gas station really the bad guy in all of this? Besides, the next day, people would begin purchasing gasoline again, and since they were still driving their cars the day before, they would be purchasing the same amounts as they would have had they filled up a day earlier.

The only way that this email would carry any weight would be if consumers stopped purchasing gasoline and oil products altogether, or if people ferociously price-compared when shopping. So far, neither of these things are happening with any regularity in North America, as consumers demand for gasoline continues to rise.

The Wooden Bowl

A frail old man went to live with his son, daughter-in-law, and four-year old grandson. The old man's hands trembled, his eyesight was blurred, and his step faltered. The family ate together at the table, but the elderly grandfather's shaky hands and failing sight made eating difficult. Peas rolled off his spoon onto the floor. When he grasped the glass, milk spilled onto the tablecloth. The son and daughter-in-law became irritated with the mess.

"We must do something about Grandfather," said the son. "I've had enough of his spilled milk, noisy eating, and food on the floor."

So the husband and wife set a small table in the corner. There, Grandfather ate alone while the rest of the family enjoyed dinner.

Since Grandfather had broken a dish or two, his food was served in a wooden bowl. When the family glanced in Grandfather's direction, he sometimes had a tear in his eye, as he sat alone. Still, the only words the couple had for him were sharp admonitions when he dropped a fork or spilled food.

The four-year-old watched it all in silence. One evening before supper, the father noticed his son playing with wood scraps on the floor.

He asked the child sweetly, "What are you making?" Just as sweetly, the boy responded, "Oh, I am making a little bowl for you and Mama to eat your food when I grow up." The four-year-old smiled and went back to work.

The words so struck the parents that they were speechless. Then tears started to stream down their cheeks. Though no words were spoken, both knew what must be done. That evening, the husband took Grandfather's hand and gently led him back to the family table. For the remainder of his days, he ate every meal with the family. And neither husband nor wife seemed to care any longer when a fork was dropped, milk spilled, or the tablecloth soiled.

On a positive note, I've learned that no matter what happens, how bad it seems today, life does go on, and it will be better tomorrow.

I've learned that you can tell a lot about a person by the way that he/she handles three things: rainy days, lost luggage, and tangled Christmas tree lights.

I've learned that regardless of your relationship with your parents, you will miss them when they're gone from your life.

I've learned that making a "living" is not the same thing as making a life.

I've learned that life sometimes gives you a second chance.

I've learned that you shouldn't go through life with a catcher's mitt on both hands. You need to be able to throw something back.

I've learned that if you pursue happiness, it will elude you. But, if you focus on your family, your friends, the needs of others, your work and doing the best you can, happiness will find you.

I've learned that whenever I decide something with an open heart, I usually make the right decision.

I've learned that even when I have pains, I don't have to be one.

I've learned that every day you should reach out and touch someone.

People love human touches, holding hands, a warm hug, or just a friendly pat on the back.

I've learned that I still have a lot to learn.

I've learned that you should pass this on to everyone you care about.

I just did.

People will forget what you said and what you did, but people will never forget how you made them feel.

Be blessed!

~ ~ ~

There aren't any real details here to verify or comment on. It is interesting to note that urban legends, even before the widespread use of email, often have an element of justice or comeuppance to them. For example, the nasty parent in the above email realizes the errors of his ways, and points them out.

September
11

The Facts About September 11

September 11, 2001 has quickly taken its place among the darkest days in American history, alongside Pearl Harbour and the John Kennedy Assassination. Like a scene from a horrific movie, thousands of people lost their lives, not because of natural disaster or invaders from space, but because radical terrorists coordinated a well-planned, surprise attack on the United States' banner city.

New York City stands out as perhaps the most recognizable city in the world. The entire free world reocognizes the United States as the most powerful nation, and New York is its commercial and business capital. Everything that is American is summed up in the Big Apple – Wall Street, The Statue of Liberty, Broadway, The Bronx, The Empire State Building, Brooklyn, the NY Yankees, and the World Trade Center.

Most people, when they think of the WTC, picture the two gleaming skyscrapers dwarfing other buildings in the Manhattan skyline. But the World Trade Center was actually made up of seven buildings altogether, nestled in the heart of Manhattan. Among the buildings were a Marriott Hotel, the Commodities Exchange and the U.S. Customs house.

The twin towers were about 1,360 feet high each. The skyscrapers were 110 stories high and over 65 yards long on the side - over half a football field long on any one side.

The World Trade Centre had been attacked before September 11; in 1993, a bomb had exploded in the parkade below the surface, killing six people.

The tragedy of September 11 shocked and horrified people not only in the U.S.A. but also around the world. The visual absurdity of two huge commercial airliners crashing into the massive towers, combined with the simultaneous assault on the Pentagon, the very symbol of U.S. military power, was nothing short of incredible. Terrorists were able to enter the United States basically without being noticed by authorities and were able to overrun the airplanes and cause massive devastation. The very freedom that the United States was proud of was one of the factors in the tragedy. The very things that define a free democracy were being taken advantage of – the freedom to move about without some authority figure looking over your shoulder. Unfortunately, security and freedom are often mutually exclusive. One usually comes at the expense of the other. And that will be one of the challenges that the United States, and the rest of the civilized world, faces in the 21st century.

Many observers spent most of September 11th watching the news, or trying to log on to their internet sites to get up-to-the-minute information. Starting pretty much on September 12th, the emails and rumours started flying. People were amazed that Nostradamus had predicted, with uncanny accuracy, the exact details of the terrorist attack. Within a few days, the infamous "tourist on the roof" photo surfaced, apparently from the wreckage and rubble. These must have been true – why would people go out of their way to fake such items?

The world is filled with all sorts of different types of people, and what some people find humorous or frivolous, other people find horrifying and despicable. It is not the purpose of this section to glorify any of the rumours or urban legends, and it is with the deepest sympathy to those families who lost loved ones that these are presented. The tragedy of September 11th brings out the very dual-nature of human beings: Onlookers watched in horror as WTC workers jumped to their deaths from 80 or 90 stories up. In the days that followed, the very same people also tuned in to the nightly news and numerous news magazine shows to watch the carnage unfold again and again. It was absolutely horrific and terrifying, yet many of us could not look away. The very best, as well as the very worst of humanity was showcased on September 11th.

Nostradamus Predictions

Subject: Nostradamus

In the City of God there will be a great thunder,
Two brothers torn apart by Chaos,
while the fortress endures,
the great leader will succumb.
The third war will begin when the big city is burning.

On the 11th day of the 9th month,
two metal birds will crash into two tall statues
in the new city,
and the world will end soon after.

In the year of the new century and nine months,
From the sky will come a great King of Terror.
The sky will burn at forty-five degrees.
Fire approaches the great new city.

In the city of York there will be a great collapse,
2 twin brothers torn apart by chaos.
While the fortress falls, the great leader will succumb.

The third big war will begin when the big city is burning.

- Nostradamus, 1654

~ ~ ~

This email "prophecy" circulated like wildfire right after the 9/11 attacks. Most of the time people would add a disclaimer such "I don't know if this is true or not, but WOW!". I was absolutely amazed that this email was as popular as it was. But the average person's need for mysticism and mystery is strong, and in the events of a tragedy, people tend to welcome interesting and incredible stories. The thought of a world just hurling through space, without a god and without any outside forces is just too much for some people to bear. That is understandable; but how much does the average person really know about Nostradamus?

If you ask one hundred people about details of Nostradamus' life, chances are you would be greeted with ninety-nine blank stares, and possibly one history professor. So what is all the fuss about, anyway?

It is not my intention to compile a huge list of facts and figures concerning Nostradamus. There are many, many books available about Nostradamus and his prophesies, and they are all intricately detailed and well-researched. However, here are some basic facts about Nostradamus that quickly undermines the credibly of the "prophetic" email.

-Nostradamus (1503-1566) lived in the 16th century.

-His real name was Michel de Nostredame. As you can tell from his name, he was French.

-He was an astrologer. This is not too be confused with astronomy, which is a branch of science. Astrology involves constellations and signs of the zodiac, whereas astronomy is hard science that involves mathematics and physics.

-Nostradamus' *Centuries* is his most famous work. It is a series of 942 verses.

-A single verse is known as a "Quatrain".

-One hundred Quatrins is called a Centurie.

The big question that immediately arises to the skeptic is this: Why are Nostradamus' writings so vague? One would think that if he had so many prophesies, and was so gifted, that he could afford to be specific as to the people, places and future events. One theory is that Nostradamus' writings were written in code to prevent his persecutions during the Inquisition. (From the "Scholars Nostradamus").

The other big question is: He wrote so many prophesies. Surely some of them must have come true. How many of his prophesies were hits and how many was he wrong about? Well, that depends on who you ask. Judging from the vastness of his writings, combined with his vague details, it would stand to reason that at least a few of them would be uncannily accurate.

All scholars, fans and researchers can do is interpret Nostradamus' writings. There were so many, and they were written so vaguely, that the major skeptic's argument is that you can take a group of quatrains and theorize that they mean anything.

For example, who is the "great leader" that Nostradamus refers to? There have been literally hundreds of leaders of major empires in our recent history. And these prophecies were written over 400 years ago, so that any major crises, plague, war or famine could be the subject of Nostradamus' writings. The laws of probability would state that eventually, at least some of Nostradamus' prophesies could be interpreted as true.

If we begin to break down the above email, the credibility of it is shattered immediately. How could Nostradamus have penned the above in 1654? After all, didn't he die in 1566? We are not off to a good start.

A few websites, such as www.truthorfiction.com and www.snopes2.com, have reported that the lines in first quatrain did not originate from Nostradamus, but actually originated from Neil Marshall, who was a student at Brock University, in Canada, in the 1990s. He wrote a paper on how Nostradamus' writings could be interpreted as many different events, since they are so vague. It appears that someone has mistaken this university student's writings as the original.

If you look at the quatrains that are in the email, but don't think about the tragedy of September 11th, and suddenly the writings appear very vague. They could be referencing any number of horrible events in the history of the world. Any fire, war or disease manages to become a possible subject for the prophecy.

There are many in depth analyses of Nostradamus' work online, as well as numerous books written about his prophesies. But the email sent around after the September 11th attacks is a twisted and distorted piece of writing, mixing in fabrication with half-truths. It is pure fiction.

The Mysterious Boyfriend

Hi All –

I think you all know that I don't normally send out hoaxes. I normally don't send out just anything that crosses my path. This one, however, is a friend of a friend and I've given it enough credibility in my mind that I'm writing it up and sending it out to all of you.

My friend's friend was dating a guy from Afghanistan up until about a month ago. She had a date with him scheduled for around September 6th and was stood up. She was understandably upset, and she went to his home to find it completely emptied.

On September 10th, she received a letter from her boyfriend explaining that he wished he could tell her why he had left and that he was sorry that it had to be like that. The part worth mentioning is that he BEGGED her not to get on any commercial airlines on 9/11 and to not go to any malls on Halloween. As soon as everything happened on the 11th, she called the FBI and has since turned over the letter.

This is not an email that I've received and decided to pass on. This came from a phone conversation with a long-time friend of mine last night.

I may be wrong, and I hope I am. However, with one of his warnings being correct and devastating, I'm not willing to take the chance on the second and wanted to make sure that people I cared about had the same information that I did.

~ ~ ~

Another variation of this email has the girlfriend receiving a warning that something horrible is going to happen on or around October 31, probably at a shopping mall. With the recent September 11th attacks still fresh in our minds, and a warning about a possible future crime, this email was very popular, and was widespread at the start of October 2001. Here is a press release from the FBI as posted on their website (http://www.fbi.gov):

U.S. Department of Justice
Federal Bureau of Investigation
For Immediate Release
October 15, 2001
Washington D.C.
FBI National Press Office

An anonymous internet electronic-mail (e-mail) message has been widely circulated pertaining to an Arab male who warned his wife not to fly on September 11, 2001 and not to go to any shopping mall on October 31, 2001. The e-mail further states that the Arab male disappeared prior to the September 11, 2001 attacks.

The FBI has conducted an inquiry into the source of this e-mail and determined that the alleged threat is not credible.

The Significant Number Eleven

The date of the attack: 9/11. 9 + 1 + 1 = 11
September 11th is the 254th day of the year. 2 + 5+ 4 = 11.
After September 11th, there are 111 days left until the end of the year.
119 is the area code for Iran and Iraq. 9 + 1+ 1 = 11.
The Twin Towers in New York City, standing side by side, look like the number 11.
The first plane to hit the towers was flight 11.
The State of New York was the 11th state added to the union.
"New York City" has 11 letters.
"Afghanistan" has 11 letters.
"The Pentagon" has 11 letters.
"Ramzi Yousef" convicted of the World Trade Centre bombing in 1993, has 11 letters.
Flight 11 had 92 people on board. 9 + 2 = 11.
Flight 77 had 65 people on board. 6 + 5 = 11.
The Muslim lunar calendar advances 11 days every year, in relation to our solar calendar.
In Numerology, the number 11 stands for challenges and strategies. In the negative sense, it stands for treachery and hidden enemies.
Timothy McVeigh was executed on June 11, 2001.
Remembrance Day is November 11th. November is also the 11th month.

~ ~ ~

It seems like there is a website for absolutely everything. One quick visit to www.countrycallingcodes.com confirmed that the details in the "Elevens" email aren't entirely true.

Actually, the country code for Iran is 98. Iraq's calling code is 964. For what its worth, Afghanistan's country code is 93. The only reason I mention Afghanistan's number is that it is the closest number to eleven so far, and that is the country that the U.S. actually retaliated against. However, I did notice that to dial a long distance number from the United States, the caller needs to dial "011" first. Strange that this wasn't mentioned in the above email.

Some people definitely enjoy finding relations and similarities where apparently none exist. To what significance any of this has to do with the real world eludes me, but it does make for interesting reading to some.

The Terrorist Attacks Were a Failure

Subject: A New Twist

By now everyone has been hearing the death toll rise and reports of the destruction from the terrorist attacks on the US. These were deplorable acts that we will never forget. But now is a time to look at the other side of the numbers coming out of New York, Washington and Pennsylvania. The sad but somewhat uplifting side that the mainstream media has not reported yet - the SURVIVAL rates and some positive news about the attacks.

The Buildings

The World Trade Center - The twin towers of the World Trade Center were places of employment for some 50,000 people. With the missing list of just over 5,000 people, that means that 90% of the people targeted survived the attack.

The Pentagon - Some 23,000 people were the target of a third plane aimed at the Pentagon. The latest count shows that only 123 lost their lives. That is an amazing 99.5% survival rate. in addition, the plane seems to have come in too low, too early to affect a large portion of the building. On top of that, the section that was hit was the first of five sections to undergo renovations that would help protect the Pentagon from terrorist attacks. It had recently completed straightening and blastproofing, saving untold lives. This attack was sad, but a statistical failure.

The Planes

American Airlines Flight 77 - This Boeing 757 that was flown into the outside of the Pentagon could have carried up to 289 people, yet only 64 were aboard. Luckily 78% of the seats were empty.

American Airlines Flight 11 - This Boeing 767 could have had up to 351 people aboard, but only carried 92. Thankfully 74% of the seats were unfilled.

United Airlines Flight 175 - Another Boeing 767 that could have sat 351 people only had 65 people on board. Fortunately it was 81% empty.

United Airlines Flight 93 - This Boeing 757 was one of the most uplifting stories yet. The smallest flight to be hijacked with only 45 people aboard out of a possible 289 had 84% of its capacity unused. Yet these people stood up to the attackers and thwarted a fourth attempted destruction of a national landmark, saving untold numbers of lives in the process.

In Summary

Out of potentially 74,280 Americans directly targeted by these inept cowards, 93% survived or avoided the attacks. That's a higher survival rate than heart attacks, breast cancer, kidney transplants and liver transplants - all common, survivable illnesses.

The Hijacked planes were mostly empty, the Pentagon was hit at it's strongest point, the overwhelming majority of people in the World Trade Center buildings escaped, and a handful of passengers gave the ultimate sacrifice to save even more lives.

Don't fear these terrorists. The odds are against them.

~ ~ ~

This email was probably sent around in response to the daily press that the mainstream media was releasing daily following the September 11th attacks. The fact of the matter was that the newspapers and daily news shows were reporting on one of the worst tragedies ever to happen to the United States, and the modern media was able to show the general public the events in graphic detail. It is human nature to try to find a positive spin on an otherwise depressing story.

There is one fallacy in the above email, however. The writer is assuming that the hijackers of the planes were trying to kill the maximum number of people possible. This is not necessarily the case. It would be more accurate to say that the terrorists were trying to kill "a significant" amount of people in order to make their message heard around the world. All in all, the September 11th attacks killed about five thousand people. But the real tragedy in the attacks lies in the everyday changes to the lives of people in the free world. In the days following the attacks, people would glance up at the skies whenever a loud plane roared overhead. Many people who worked in high-rise skyscrapers took stress leave. Untold numbers of friends and family members were horrified and shocked by the attacks.

These were the real goals of the terrorists- not murdering 6,000 people, but rather the symbolic destruction of the United States capital and military centers. The fact that the planes were not filled to capacity is, at best, a lucky coincidence. But that's all that it is. Luck.

One can look at the attacks and see the number of lives that were spared – it was true that the aircraft were only partially filled and that the World Trade Center was hit early in the morning, before it was filled with tourists and businesspeople. But, on the other hand, one can also see the complete devastation that occurred. Every single one of the passengers and crew aboard every one of the four hijacked planes were killed. And virtually every person that was inside the twin towers when they collapsed were killed. In those instances, the death rate was virtually 100%.

The hijackers and terrorists probably never expected the entire World Trade Center to collapse, or to wreak havoc on the Pentagon. No doubt they succeeded beyond their wildest expectations. The sad reality is that the hijackers probably achieved their main goal: to create unease and the feeling that no one is safe, anywhere in the free world.

I point out the negative aspects of the attacks with some reluctance; the spirit of the above email is positive, and it is obvious that the author is trying to raise hopes of people who may be depressed or scared. And there is nothing wrong with trying to accentuate the positive in an otherwise tragic situation.

NASA Photographs From Space

Subject: FW: Tonight

10:30 EASTERN TIME -- 9:30 Central -- 8:30 Mountain -- 7:30 Pacific
I just heard on the radio that the U.S. has asked that everyone step out on their lawns tonight at 10:30 and light a candle. They will be taking a satellite picture of the U.S. and posting it on the news tomorrow morning. Please pass this on to as many people as possible.

~ ~ ~

Subject: Candle Lighting Tonight

A formal request from NASA:
10:30 EASTERN TIME, 9:30 Central, 8:30 >Mountain, 7:30 Pacific

NASA has asked that everyone step out on their lawns tonight at 10:30 and light a candle. They will be positioning a satellite to take a picture of the U.S. and posting it on the news tomorrow morning.

Please pass this on to as many people as possible.

~ ~ ~

As you can see, internet urban legends tend to change and evolve as they are passed from person to person. These emails (and other, similar ones) were sent around in the days following the September 11ᵗʰ attacks. The details, such as the date and time of the candle-lighting varied as the email circulated around. A nice gesture to be sure. However, it is highly doubtful that candlelight would be visible from a wide-angle, photograph of the entire U.S.A.

There are a few holes in this email. For example, at 7:30 pacific time, it is still light out on the west coast. Wouldn't it be better to light candles outside when it is dark? Also, even if we assume that every American stepped out of their homes, all at the same time, then all electric lights in every city would have to be shut off in order for candlelight to be visible. This would include all the lights in your house, all streetlights and traffic lights, electric signs, and the like, in every city and town in the region.

NASA did not issue this email. NASA did pay tribute to the victims of the September 11ᵗʰ attacks, but it was in a different form than candles. Here is a copy of a December press release from NASA's website (http://www.nasa.gov):

SHUTTLE, STATION CREW MEMBERS TO HONOR SEPTEMBER 11 VICTIMS

NOTE TO EDITORS: N01-74 SHUTTLE, STATION CREWMEMBERS TO HONOR SEPTEMBER 11 VICTIMS

As part of a nationwide tribute to those who lost their lives in the September 11th attacks on America, crewmembers aboard Space Shuttle Endeavour and the International Space Station will mark the three-month anniversary of the attacks tomorrow, Tuesday, Dec. 11, 2001, at 8:46 a.m. EST.

The tribute is part of the continuing coverage of the STS-108 mission. The tribute, which will be carried on NASA Television, is expected to include the playing of the U.S. and Russian national anthems in the Space Shuttle and International Space Station Mission Control Centers at NASA's Johnson Space Center in Houston. Remarks from the three commanders and the playing of a taped tribute from the ten crewmembers aboard the space shuttle and orbiting space station will also be included in tomorrow's event.

Endeavour is orbiting the Earth with 6000 small American flags that are part of the agency's "Flags for Heroes and Families" program. Also aboard the shuttle are three large U.S. and Marine Corps flags, which were flying at the World Trade Center, the Pentagon and the Pennsylvania State Capitol, along with a number of New York City police officer shields and patches, a Fire Department of New York flag and a poster with the pictures of firefighters who lost their lives in the attacks.

NASA TV is available on GE-2, Transponder 9C at 85 degrees West longitude, vertical polarization, with a frequency of 3880 MHz, and audio of 6.8 MHz.

The Tourist Photograph

FW: FREAKY

This picture was from a camera found in the wreckage of the WTC, developed by the FBI for evidence and released on the net today... the guy still has no name and is missing.

~ ~ ~

This particular e-mail is by far the most controversial and upsetting to many people. And, of course, it was the most widely sent.

The fact of the matter is that people enjoy scaring each other. You can see it when a six-year-old jumps out in the hallway and scares his mother, or you can see it when we sit around the campfire in the middle of the eerie night and tell spooky stories. This is nothing new.

But is the picture real? Upon closer scrutiny, it quickly becomes evident that the picture is completely false. On the internet, there are entire web pages devoted to examining the picture in exhaustive detail, noting the angles of light, the digital imaging and the like. However, a few blatant errors come to light that basically render the photograph a fraud quite quickly.

The north World Trade Centre tower had a huge, 360-foot television mast, and no observation tower. Since our tourist is standing on the observation deck on the roof, then by the powers of elimination, he must be standing on Building 2 of the World Trade Centre, also known as the south tower, which did in fact have an observation deck, 110 stories up.

The flight that hit the south tower was Flight 175, and it impacted the south tower at about 9 a.m. EST. Flight 175 was a Boeing 767, approached from the south side, and impacted the southern face of Building 2.

The observation deck on WTC 2 opened up at 9:30 a.m. But the plane hit WTC 2 at 9 a.m. This would mean that the observation deck was not open to tourists when the picture was supposedly taken.

The weather on September 11th in Manhattan was warm (about 70° F). Yet our tourist is wearing a knit cap and a heavy winter jacket.

Usually with non-professional cameras, the focus of the picture must either be up close or far away. It is highly unusual to have the tourist (barely 10 feet away) and the plane both in perfect focus. Remember, the tourist is standing still, while the aircraft is travelling nearly 300 mph. This leads us to believe that the plane was taken from another picture and added in.

Perhaps the most compelling piece of evidence is that the plane in the tourist photo is a Boeing 757. However, both Flights 11 and 175 were, in reality, Boeing 767s. The aircraft in the photo and the aircraft that were used in the attacks are entirely different.

There are some other puzzling aspects to this story. The entire World Trade Center was absolutely destroyed, yet we are to believe that a camera survived a 110-story fall, was picked out of a mound of rubble surrounded by sharp shards of concrete and support beams, and yet the film survived intact.

Also, according to the message in the email, the FBI released this photograph after scouring it for evidence. What would the FBI possibly be checking this camera for? It seems unlikely, but let's assume for the sake of argument that the FBI indeed did check the camera. Why would they release the photo onto the internet? An image like this, if it was real, would surely serve only to make the public gasp in horror. It would not add anything to forward the investigation. And assuming that the FBI did in fact release this photograph, would it really be making its rounds on the internet? Why wouldn't they release it through a news conference? It would easily have been the headlining story for every national television news show, as well as on the front page of every newspaper in the free world.

This is the original photograph of the aircraft, as taken by Jonathan Derden and posted on www.Airliners.net. (Photo copyright Jonathan Derden and used with permission).

There is a website called "Tourist of Death" (http://www.touristofdeath.com) that features galleries of the WTC tourist in other situations. An entire culture of people devoted to fixing photographs with the "Tourist of Death" is operating in full force online, for better or for worse. These doctored photos put the tourist in front of volcanoes and other disasters throughout history. While some of them are highly-skilled photographic alternations, others are simply "cut and paste" jobs with the tourist plunked in front of the disaster. The quality of the photographs (technically speaking) varies substantially.

But just who is this tourist, anyway?

Originally a Brazilian, named Jose Roberto Penteado, claimed to be the WTC tourist. WIRED magazine online (http://www.wired.com) reported in a November 9, 2001 article that Jose apparently had the photos to prove it. While Jose was enjoying media attention, the friends of the real WTC tourist came forward to "Index," which is a Hungarian online news site.

About two weeks later (on November 20, 2001), WIRED magazine online (http://www.wired.com) reported that they had reason to believe that the original WTC tourist was not Jose Roberto Penteado, but rather a guy named "Peter" from Hungary. (Peter did not want his last name revealed, as he wishes to keep his anonymity).

The basic story is that Peter sent the original doctored photo to his friends, and he thought that it would end there. He did it as a joke. Apparently, his friends thought that the photo was so good that they forwarded it on to some other friends, who did the same. Peter is amazed that the photograph circled the entire world and has now become a permanent fixture in internet lore.

Q33NY

Subject: Q33NY – Wingdings

Check this out – if you type the name of the flight number for one of the planes that crashed into the World Trade Centre as follows:

Q33NY

and then highlight the text, and change it to "Wingdings" font... see what happens! Creepy.

~ ~ ~

I'm not quite sure what the significance of the "wingdings" font has to do with extreme terrorists from the third world. But when you do in fact type in "Q33NY" and then convert it to wingdings font, this emerges:

The big problem with this email is that "Q33NY" was not a flight number for either one of the New York planes. The flight numbers of the aircraft that hit the World Trade Centre towers were Flight 11 and Flight 175.

However, another "wingdings" experiment is to type in the letters "NYC" and change it to Wingdings. You get this:

Bin Laden and the Soft Drinks

Subject: Osama Bin Laden

Everyone might be wondering, "How does this colossal prick manage to amass such a great amount of money to be able to mount an operation such as September 11th?"

Let's get enlightened. Gum arabic is used in the manufacture of tons of products that we Americans consume in gigantic quantities, such as soft drinks.

Well, it so happens that BIN LADEN is one of the primary owners of the company based in Sudan which produces Gum arabic. So, we have basically been stuffing money his pockets.

Do the world a favour: start reading the labels of products you buy, and DON'T BUY ANYTHING WITH GUM ARABIC IN IT. Yes girls, that means NO MORE DIET SODAS. This ingredient is used in desserts, too. Maybe it'll put a dent in the monster's pockets, and he won't be such a welcome guest in the communities that harbour him.

Circulate this sucker around the world. IT AIN'T NO HOAX FOLKS

~ ~ ~

It is scary to think that by purchasing a soft drink or other consumer product, you are actually contributing to Bin Laden's profits. However, according to the National Soft Drink Association (http://www.ndsa.org), the U.S. state department has intimated that they have no evidence to suggest that Bin Laden has any financial ties to the Sudanese gum arabic industry.

(Read the full press release at http://www.nsda.org/About/news/

gumarabic.html). The NSDA goes on to say that U.S. companies must obtain approval from the U.S. government in order to use gum arabic from Sudan.

A 1998 article in *The Baltimore Sun* reported that Bin Laden divested himself financially from any Sudanese Gum Arabic holdings that he might have had back in 1996. The Gum Arabic Company of Sudan Ltd., which controls the export of the product worldwide, has denied repeatedly any involvement with Bin Laden.

Israel and the Soft Drinks

Subject: Coca-Cola and Israel
I have heard various rumours about the nature of the relationship between Coca-Cola and the State of Israel. I recently heard that NBC stated that "the income that Coca-Cola will get in the coming 4 days starting from Monday will be donated to Israel."

~ ~ ~

Coca-Cola operates in over 200 countries and is a multinational economic corporation. On their own website (http://www2.coca-cola.com), Coca-Cola is quick to point out that the above email rumour is simply not true.

From Coca-Cola's website:

Our Response: These rumours are false. The Coca-Cola Company does not support or oppose governments, political or religious causes and does not take a stance on issues that do not directly affect the soft drink industry.
Coca-Cola shares are owned by people from all over the world, as Coca-Cola is a publicly traded company on the New York Stock Exchange and NASDAQ.

Oliver North vs. Osama Bin Laden

THE YEAR WAS 1987!

At a lecture the other day they were playing an old news video clip of Lt. Col. Oliver North testifying at the Iran-Contra hearings during the Reagan Administration. There was Ollie in front of God and country getting the third degree, but what he said was stunning! He was being drilled by some senator. "Did you not recently spend close $60,000 for a home security system?"

Ollie replied, "Yes, I did, sir." The senator continued, trying to get a laugh out of the audience. "Isn't that just a little excessive?"

"No, sir," continued Ollie.

"No? And why not?" the senator asked.

"Because the lives of my family and I were threatened, sir."

"Threatened? By whom?" the senator questioned.

"By a terrorist, sir." Ollie answered.

"Terrorist? What terrorist could possibly scare you that much?"

"His name is Osama bin Laden, sir." Ollie replied.

At this point the senator tried to repeat the name, but couldn't pronounce it, which most people back then probably couldn't. A couple of people laughed at the attempt. Then the senator continued. "Why are you so afraid of this man?" the senator asked.

"Because, sir, he is the most evil person alive that I know of," Ollie answered.

"And what do you recommend we do about him?" asked the senator.

"Well, sir, if it was up to me, I would recommend that an assassin team be formed to eliminate him and his men from the face of the earth." The senator disagreed with this approach, and that was all that was shown of the clip.

By the way, the Senator was Al Gore! What year was it again? Some people just don't listen when they should!

~ ~ ~

This email has been making the rounds, and if it seems outrageous, it is because it is. It is completely factually incorrect. Al Gore did not participate in the Iran Contra hearings in 1987. It is also important to note that in 1987, Osama Bin Laden was not labeled a terrorist by the United States, or anyone else for that matter. Bin Laden was fighting Russians in Afghanistan. The terrorist that Oliver North was referring to in the hearings was Abu Nidal, not Osama Bin Laden.

Beware The Words Of Julius Caesar

Subject: Caesar
Beware the leader who bangs the drums of war in order to whip the citizenry into a patriotic fervour, for patriotism is indeed a double-edged sword. It both emboldens the blood, just as it narrows the mind.
And when the drums of war have reached a fever pitch and the blood boils with hate and the mind has closed, the leader will have no need in seizing the rights of the citizenry. Rather, the citizenry, infused with fear and blinded by patriotism, will offer up all of their rights unto the leader and gladly so.
How do I know? For this is what I have done. And I am Caesar.

~ ~ ~

This email has been floating around since the September 11th attacks, usually in response to the United States' military policy. Sometimes it is attributed to Julius Caesar himself, and sometimes William Shakespeare gets the credit for the writing. But either way, it would appear that these words were not written by either man.

I do not claim to be an expert on Shakespeare by any stretch of the imagination. However, I do understand that he wrote his plays in Iambic Pentameter. This would mean that the words flow with accents, much like hard notes in music. For example:

To be, or not to be, that is the question:
Whether 'tis nobler in the mind to suffer

The slings and arrows of outrageous fortune
Or to take arms against a sea of troubles,
And by opposing end them?

--From Hamlet (III, i, 56-61)

Would read out loud:

To BE or NOT to BE, that IS the QUESTION:
WHEther tis NOBler IN the MIND to SUFfer
the SLINGS and ARRows OF outRAGEous FORtune
OR to TAKE arms aGAINST a SEA of TROUBles
and BY opPOSing END them?

Mostly it is a "duh DUH duh DUH duh DUH" kind of rhythm, although sometimes the heavy accent (DUH) comes before the small accent (duh). There's a certain cadence and rhythm to Shakespeare's writings that create a completely different experience when read aloud, as opposed to reading them on the page. Of course, you wouldn't stress certain syllables with an exaggerated accent; when reading the words, they tend to flow naturally and eloquently. When the above email is read again with Iambic Pentameter in mind, it just doesn't flow very well.

But my opinion on how well the email sounds is, admittedly, just an opinion. You can visit the Shakespeare play Julius Caesar in its entirety at http://www.allshakespeare.com. I searched the play and could find no evidence of the "drums of war" quote in Julius Caesar. In fact, I could not locate the "drums of war" lines in any Shakespeare play.

Not So Funny Money

SUBJECT: INCREDIBLE

INCREDIBLE THINGS HAPPEN IN AMERICA...

1) Fold a $20 bill in half.

2) Fold again, taking care to fold it exactly as below

3) Fold the other end, exactly as before
LOOK - the PENTAGON is on fire!!

4) Now, simply turn it over. THE TWIN TOWERS ARE ABLAZE!

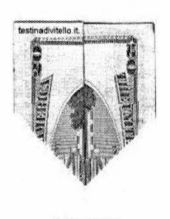 

What a coincidence! A simple geometric fold creates a catastrophic premonition printed on all $20 bills!
COULD IT GET ANY WORSE?
YES! Look at this!

A TRIPLE COINCIDENCE ON A SIMPLE $20 BILL

EVEN MORE PROOF: 9 + 11 = 20

~ ~ ~

It is hard to argue with stunning visual evidence such as this. Or is it really that stunning? Upon first glance, these tricks with the U.S. twenty may dazzle you and your friends. But if we dig a bit further, some of the extraordinary coincidences are not that amazing. For example, the "Pentagon" and "Twin Towers" that are seemingly depicted on the money are not really those buildings, they just happen to resemble them if you twist and fold the money that way. Either you are the type of person who believes that this is merely "fun with money," or someone who wants to believe that there is some sort of weird mojo magic that connects U.S. currency with the events of September 11th.

In all fairness, most people on the web seem to agree that it is merely a coincidence, and that someone (possibly an Origami specialist) with way too much time on their hands managed to come up with some interesting ways to amuse themselves.

More U.S. Dollar Conspiracies?

If you fold a five-dollar bill and a ten-dollar bill the same as the twenty, the five shows you the towers *before* the attack and the ten shows the towers *after* the first hit. COINCIDENCE?

 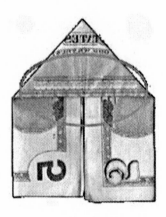

The ten shows the towers after the first hit. Notice the building in the foreground - you will see that it's in the picture and on the bill!

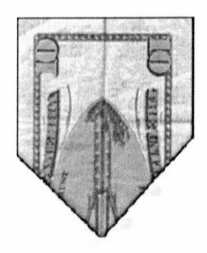 

Fold a $50 using the same method as before.

And finally the $100 note.

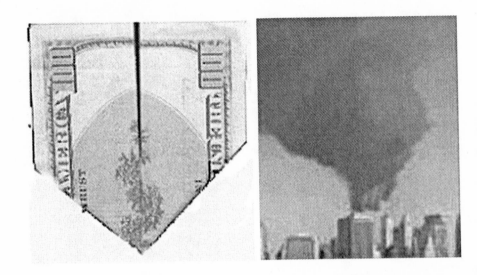

~ ~ ~

Again, either you enjoy this sort of thing or you don't. With the popularity of the "twenty-dollar bill coincidence," people inevitably ran to their wallets to see if they could find anything of interest on any other denominations. Since there were so many different aspects of the September 11th attack, it is not incredibly surprising that some were found. Some of the "coincidences" are a little more impressive than others, but they all supposedly depict representations, not actual buildings or events.

Trick Or Treat - Or Just A Trick?

Subject: Danger At Halloween
Last week a gentleman of middle eastern descent opened up an account at the Hackensack, NJ Costco and purchased close to $7,000 worth of candy. I guess this was not particularly alarming because many small businesses purchase large amounts of items at Costco. What became alarming was that this same person (or someone using this person's card) purchased close to $15,000 worth of additional candy two days ago at the Wayne Costco.

The cashier became alarmed at this large purchase of candy and was even more concerned when the person paid cash. I'm told she was fearful and did not alert anyone in the store until after the person had left, and then she reported it to authorities.

I pass this along in case your children or grandchildren go trick or treating. I do not know the intentions of the person who purchased all this candy, but in today's time I do not think it is crazy to be overly cautious. The possibility of this candy being tainted and resold to unknowing discount distributors and then passed on to unknowing consumers is too great.

~ ~ ~

The age-old scare at Halloween is the same - your innocent children are going to come home from stranger's porches with a bag full of candy, and there is no way that you can be sure that it is safe to eat. It would appear that this story is another attempt to scare parents at Halloween. Or is it?

This is a relatively new urban legend that is based on truth. There was an incident in October 2001 where a middle-eastern man did in fact buy a large quantity of candy from a Hackensack, NJ Costco. The FBI had investigated this case and it was determined that he bought the candy for resale purposes. The FBI did not reveal the nationality of the man, and they have no evidence that the man was a terrorist or had any malicious plans with the candy.

This legend, although somewhat new, will no doubt be circulated next year, and the year after that. After all, the chances of Middle-Eastern people purchasing large amounts of candy somewhere in North America during October are rather good.

Conclusion

We have seen some emails that were designed to scare you, some that were designed to make you laugh, and some that were just plain weird. We all have some friends who love to send you emails. Some people hardly ever forward (FW:) anything. Why is that?

Some people are really annoyed by urban legends. Are you one of them? Do you read these kinds of emails and immediately discard them? Or you do pour over them, take them to heart, and forward them along to three or four (or twenty) of your closest friends?

And if so... why do we forward these emails on to our friends and family, anyway? The most obvious answer is that email is a convenient and easy way to pass along information. Can you imagine printing off an interesting story and addressing some envelopes and mailing your friends and family these stories? Chances are that the labour involved would outweigh any potential benefits. However, with modern technology, we are able to forward emails literally at the speed of light. At times we all enjoy a good scare or an uplifting story, but sometimes the emails can be an unwelcome addition to an already loaded inbox.

Many of the emails seems to be written by someone with too much time on their hands. Just what are they trying to accomplish anyway? It is interesting to note that many of the emails and warnings that float around in cyberspace are designed to help us, however misguided some of them may be. Most people inherently enjoy helping others, and try to make the world a better place. There are a few exceptions, however; one can only wonder how the fake tourist photograph of the WTC plane is helping anyone. But it is in these most controversial emails that our true human nature comes out.

People enjoy helping each other, but we also enjoy scaring others, and getting creeped out ourselves. Its exciting and interesting to be scared, or to hear about others who have gone through horrible ordeals. And we enjoy telling or sharing a good story. It's been that way since the first tribes sat around fires, draped in skins and telling tales to celebrate the day's adventures. These stories continue on, the medium changing from verbal to electric. Emails represent the latest evolution in the age-old tradition of humans- to tell a good story first, and if it is true, well then, so much the better.

It's one thing to enjoy a good urban legend as a story, but it is also important to not believe everything that you read. Many of these emails are just simply made up. They are not true. There is something about seeing words in print that tend to create an aura of respectability and truth. We are programmed in our lives to believe the written word, because there is an underlying logic that assumes that if someone had to go to the trouble to create an email, or article, or television report, or newspaper piece about a story, why would they lie? However, there are many "spins" on stories that contort the truth. Truth is very subjective, and slight exaggerations tend to distort the underlying kernels of truth that might have started out in any of the urban legends that are circulated around. And some of them are quite simply made up.

Remember to enjoy a good story, but keep in mind that the internet and emails are full of people just like you and me, who are capable of lying... and telling the truth.

Bibliography

- Anecdotes and Legends, Press Releases. [Online] Available from Centers for Disease Control and Prevention, http://www.cdc.gov 2002.

- Anecdotes and Legends. [Online] Available from City of Dallas Police Department, http://www.dallaspolice.net 2002.

- Anecdotes and Legends. [Online] Available http://www.snopes.com 2002.

- Anecdotes and Legends. [Online] Available http://www.snopes2.com 2002.

- Anecdotes and Legends. [Online] Available http://www.symantec.com 2003.

- Anecdotes and Legends. [Online] Available http://www.truthorfiction.com 2002.

- Anecdotes and Legends. [Online] Available http://www.urbanlegends.com 2002.

- Anecdotes and Legends. [Online] Available http://www.touristofdeath.com 2002.

- Animal Poison Control Center Toxicology Bulletins: Febreze Fabric Refresher UpdateFriday, January 11, 2002 from ASPCA website, found at http://www.aspca.org, 2002.

- Background Information on September 11th / 2002 Attacks in the U.S.A. [Online] Available at CSICOP http://www.csicop.org/hoaxwatch 2002.

- Boycott Israel Campaign, from http://www.inminds.co.uk/boycott-coca-cola.html website, 2002.

- Censor M.S., Alexander. "Don't Believe The Hype." *Smart Computing* November 2001: p. 31.

- Chaplin, Heather. "Urban Health Legends." *Fitness* October 2000: p. 58.

- Facts on Abraham Lincoln and Family. [Online] Available from "Abraham Lincoln: An Educational Site, http://www.geocities.com/ SunsetStrip/Venue/5217/lincoln.html 2002.

- Facts on Abraham Lincoln and Family. [Online] Available from "Damaged Transmission | Kennedy vs. Lincoln, http://dtonline.jaguar7926.com/misc/linken.html 2002.

- Hickman, Leo. Tracking Down The Tourist Of Death. [Online] from *The Guardian,* available at http://www.guardian.co.uk November 30, 2001.

- Johnston, L.A. "Cyberconspiracy Theories". [Online] http://www.post-gazette.com/magazine/19980730bsocial1.asp. July 30, 1998.

- Jone and friends. Jack Daniel's Tennessee Whisky. http://www.jackdaniels.com 2002.

- Public Domain Photographs. Available at NOAA Photo Library http://www.photolib.noaa.gov 2002.

- Public Domain Photographs. Available at http://freewebgrafix.com 2002.

- Richard, Jeff. Safety Tips, specifically computer viruses. [Online] Available from Jeff Richard's Virus and Netlore, http://hoaxinfo.com 2002.

- Safety Tips. [Online] Available from City of Chicago Police Department, http://www.ci.chi.il.us/CommunityPolicing 2002.

- Safety Tips. [Online] Available from City of Windsor Police Department, http://www.police.windsor.on.ca 2002.

- Trimble, Vance H. *Overnight Success: Federal Express & Frederick Smith, Its Renegade Creator*, published by Crown Publishers.

Printed in the United States
23747LVS00005B/150